Earth Bible Commentary

Series Editor
Norman C. Habel

PRAISE FOR *JONAH: AN EARTH BIBLE COMMENTARY*

'In true islander fashion, Jione Havea surrenders the book of Jonah to an interpretive rip current that takes readers far from the beaches and beaching of traditional commentary. Salty, sandy, and saturated with stories, the wayward book lures us to watery domains where boats, boat people, and contaminated fish float in life-threatening limbo; casts us ashore on ancestral grounds where bushes, behemoth, and bustling cities confront our present climate crisis; and forces us to linger and look around in imperilled places where Jonah, Yhwh, the narrator, and most commentators are reluctant to go.'

— Danna Nolan Fewell, Drew University, United States

'As editor of the Earth Bible Commentary series, I have encouraged writers to pursue a radical reorientation. But Havea's work goes beyond past efforts. It is not simply that he is an islander who identifies with the ocean and its world; he swirls the reader forward between impulses connected with God, Jonah, the fish and Nineveh. Then, when we meet the beasts in the last line of the book, he swirls us backwards to discover new dimensions of this classic ancient "satire." He even writes his work for "normal readers" to enjoy.'

— Normal Habel, Flinders University, Australia

'Jione Havea's commentary on Jonah is astonishingly fresh – fresh enough to make one smell salty wind on the sea. By interweaving his scholarly ingenuity, artistic imagination, islander experiences and activist commitment, Havea performs his retelling of the story of Jonah, moving back and forth in the narrative, looking beyond the characters of Jonah and God, and animating other earthed and inanimate subjects. In the present age of ecological crisis and climate injustices, this troubled and troubling reading of Jonah invites readers to flow and fly across cultures beyond the limits of textuality and the conventional interpretations promoted by Western anthropocentricism and individualism. This commentary is useful not only for students of the Bible but also anyone who is interested in social, global, eco-justice as well as interfaith dialogue. I absolutely recommend it.'

— Jin Young Choi, Colgate Rochester Crozer Divinity School, United States

JONAH

An Earth Bible Commentary

Jione Havea

LONDON • NEW YORK • OXFORD • NEW DELHI • SYDNEY

T&T CLARK
Bloomsbury Publishing Plc
50 Bedford Square, London, WC1B 3DP, UK
1385 Broadway, New York, NY 10018, USA
29 Earlsfort Terrace, Dublin 2, Ireland

BLOOMSBURY, T&T CLARK and the T&T Clark logo are trademarks of
Bloomsbury Publishing Plc

First published in Great Britain 2020
This paperback edition published in 2021

Copyright © Jione Havea, 2020

Jione Havea has asserted his right under the Copyright, Designs and
Patents Act, 1988, to be identified as Author of this work.

For legal purposes the Acknowledgement on p. ix constitutes an extension
of this copyright page.

Cover design: Charlotte James
Cover image © borchee/istock

All rights reserved. No part of this publication may be reproduced or transmitted
in any form or by any means, electronic or mechanical, including photocopying,
recording, or any information storage or retrieval system, without prior
permission in writing from the publishers.

Bloomsbury Publishing Plc does not have any control over, or responsibility for, any
third-party websites referred to or in this book. All internet addresses given in this
book were correct at the time of going to press. The author and publisher regret
any inconvenience caused if addresses have changed or sites have ceased to
exist, but can accept no responsibility for any such changes.

A catalogue record for this book is available from the British Library.

Library of Congress Control Number: 2019956623

ISBN: HB: 978-0-5676-7454-8
PB: 978-0-5677-0481-8
ePDF: 978-0-5676-7455-5
eBook: 978-0-5676-9377-8

Series: Earth Bible Commentary

Typeset by Deanta Global Publishing Services, Chennai, India

To find out more about our authors and books visit www.bloomsbury.com and
sign up for our newsletters.

CONTENTS

List of Figures	vi
Preface	vii
Acknowledgement	ix

Chapter 1
COMMENTARY FLOWS 1

Part I
FLOWING FORWARD

Chapter 2
FLOW INTO THE SEA (JON. 1.1–2.10) 19

Chapter 3
FLOW INTO NINEVEH (JON. 2.10–4.11) 35

Part II
FLOWING BACKWARD

Chapter 4
BEASTS THAT MATTERED (JON. 4.10-11) 55

Chapter 5
A BUSH THAT MOVED (JON. 4.1-9) 68

Chapter 6
A CITY THAT BELIEVED (JON. 3.1-10) 80

Chapter 7
A FISH THAT VOMITED (JON. 1.17–2.10) 92

Chapter 8
A BOAT THAT THOUGHT (JON. 1.4-16) 104

Chapter 9
A FLIGHT THAT CONTINUES (JON. 1.1-3) 116

A POSTSCRIPT 127

References	131
Scriptural Characters Index	135
Scriptural Reference Index	137

FIGURES

1.1	Donatus S. Moulo Moiwend, *Guardian of the Palm Leaves* (oil on palm leaf, 2010)	4
1.2	Donatus S. Moulo Moiwend, *Tree of Life* (oil on bark, undated)	5
1.3	Family tree	6
1.4	Emmanuel Garibay, *Akademiko* (oil on board, 2009)	10
3.1	Emmanuel Garibay, *My Way* (oil on board, 2009)	41
4.1	Youngsolwarans, *Where's the key?* (oil on canvas, 2014)	66
8.1	A home flooded by rising sea level at South Tarawa, Kiribati (2019)	111
8.2	Emmanuel Garibay, *Prusisyon* (oil on canvas, 2009)	113

PREFACE

Climate change, a devastating reality in and of the current time, is an opportunity to reconsider the significance of biblical texts for life situations and struggles, which differ between different contexts, as well as the purposes and practices of biblical commentary. The book of Jonah, which has been explained by so many commentators over so many years in so many (is)lands, and the ecological drives of the Earth Bible Commentary (EBC) series, provides me with this opportunity (and excuse) to rethink, repent (as did God in Jon. 3.10) and tap (into) the flows of the commentary (as traditionally understood) business. This EBC volume takes advantage of this opportunity in two ways: first, by reading the Jonah narrative forward, giving special attention to the orientation of the narrative towards the sea and (looking back from the hinterland) towards Nineveh, and then reading the same narrative backward, highlighting the difference that sea and native (is)land matters make to rereading the biblical narrative. And second, by not buying into the narrator's obsession with Jonah and his God, as if they are the only characters who matter in the narrative. Sea, wind, boat, fish, city, hinterland, sun, bush, worm and beasts—which are earth(ed) characters in the book of Jonah—also have roles and voices in this narrative and they matter in this commentary.

My drive in this EBC work is not to repeat what other humans say about the book of Jonah (so this commentary lacks a literature review, some of which are repeated and engaged in my previous publications on Jonah, but references are given to works that give further explanations of or alternative views to the readings proposed), but to reflect on the significance of earth(ed) subjects in and for the narrative. This is therefore not a traditional commentary in the Western academic sense, but a commentary that has been traditioned in the native sense— it is a commentary with land, sea, underworld and native (is)land orientations. Politically, this EBC work seeks to be relevant for *normal readers* as well. My sense of who and what are normal is generous, for my obsession is not to please only the scholarly authorities but to also provide a platform upon which academic, church, community, labour and activist interests may intersect.

The work on this commentary was assisted by many organizations and friends. The Council for World Mission supported me through the Discernment and Radical Engagement (DARE) programme, thanks to the faith and hospitality of Sudipta Singh. Trinity Methodist Theological College (Auckland, Aotearoa New Zealand), Public and Contextual Theology research centre (PaCT) of Charles Sturt University (Australia), Society of Asian Biblical Studies (SABS), Oceania Biblical Studies Association (OBSA) and Society of Biblical Literature (SBL) were the research "boats" that i boarded during this work. Many of the views presented in this commentary were inspired by *talanoa* (stories, tellings, conversations) of and with normal people in prison and around kava circles (especially Parklea prison and the Fōfōʻanga kava clubs). This commentary therefore comes out of and goes out towards a rainbow of interests and readerships. To the many friends and critics in those collectives, and for the many people who have patiently supported me over the years, I give my soulful gratitude. I cannot name all of you, for i will miss some, but i respect and appreciate your contributions to this work.

To all whose paths i have crossed, pardon my naming four women whose departure (by death) and continuing presence (in faith) keep my feet on the ground and occasionally in the deep: Sela Kakala and Lūʻisa Lākai have boarded the boats of the ancestors, while Monica Jyotsna and Diya Lākai help me find distractions in the storms of living. *Sai tau feke!*

ACKNOWLEDGEMENT

The work on this book was kindly supported by Council for World Mission.

Chapter 1

COMMENTARY FLOWS

A largely unspoken expectation in biblical scholarship is for a Bible commentary to locate and explain a biblical book in accordance with the assumed intentions of the author(s) and the sociopolitical world(s) in which the book was written (see Ben Zvi 2003; Handy 2007), noting how the purposes for and meanings of the book may have changed or taken new shapes when that book was edited, redacted, canonized, translated and interpreted in religious and secular settings (see Limburg 1993: 99–123; Jenson 2008; Caspi and Greene 2011; Bob 2013). It is thus expected that the author(s) of a Bible commentary dive into and through the rhetoric of the book to explain how its parts relate to each other, to resolve textual problems, to reconcile translation variances, to determine the histories behind and in the book, and to survey the scholarly literature on that book. On those matters, a mainline Bible commentary is expected to offer a set of critical notes and reasonable explanations that determine original meanings and assert correct interpretations.[1]

With respect to the book of Jonah, despite its brevity, the array of commentaries and scholarly literature is voluminous and varied. The reception history of the book is dense and heavy extending from the shadows of Eden (see Berger 2016) onto the canvases of artists, the winks of satirists (see McKenzie 2005: 1–21), the directions of ethicists (see De La Torre 2007), the shelves of adult and children literature as well as to toys, computer games and the big screen (see Sherwood 2000). At different times, new and novel approaches to biblical criticism have been trialled with Jonah,[2] but not all creative and critical approaches find the book of Jonah appealing or relevant. This broad range has a lot to say about readers as well (see Lasine 2016; on implied and actual readers of Jonah, see Person Jr. 1996: 90–163).

---

1. On Jonah, see the commentaries by Gabriël Cohn (1969), Hans Walter Wolff (1977), Jack M. Sasson (1990), James Limburg (1993) and Uriel Simon (1999).

2. For examples of how Jonah has been read through the lenses of literary criticism, see Magonet (1983); psychoanalysis, see LaCocque & LaCocque (1990); poetics and interpretation, see Craig (1993); conversation analysis, see Person Jr. (1996); reception history, see Sherwood (2000); cognition, syntax and semantics, see Kamp (2004); social sciences, see Handy (2007); intertextuality, see Muldoon (2010); queer commentary, see Carden (2006); trauma theory, see Boase and Agnew (2016).

What new insights then could an Earth Bible Commentary (EBC) add to the study of Jonah?[3] And why should i,[4] whose first response is usually to flee from the business of Bible commentaries, write this EBC volume?

My response to the second question is simple, following Norman Habel's lead, because the EBC series "requires a radical re-orientation to the biblical text" (Habel 2011: 3). I did not flee from this assignment because, appropriating images from the Jonah narrative, it is an opportunity for me to throw the commentary genre into the stormy seas of reading.[5] Time will tell what impact this attempt might have and if the minders (or gods) of the commentary business will send a huge fish to rescue the commentary genre, but this EBC volume seeks to embrace the opportunities that wait from the hinterland of Nineveh. My orientation towards and beyond Nineveh is not because that was the place where God wanted Jonah to go, or because Nineveh was a godforsaken place (see Lindsay 2016). Rather, i am interested in Nineveh because there were beasts there that had something to teach God (and this becomes clear only at the end of the narrative, Jon. 4.10-11) and readers about life and rescue. It is for this reason that in this commentary, in the company of David Clines (1995, 1998) and David Jobling (1998), i read Jonah forward (in the direction of the Hebrew text, right to left) in Chapters 2–3, and then backward (left to right) in Chapters 4–9. Ideologically, this EBC volume flows both ways.

Reading Jonah in both directions problematizes the traditional textual parameters and linear readerly orientations that mainline critics place upon the narrative. One of the inspirations for this bi-textual flow is David Jobling's commentary on 1 Samuel. Jobling subverts the way that "the canonical division exerts tremendous pressure on scholars to read the beginning of 1 Samuel as a new beginning—to read it *forward* [into 2 Samuel] rather than *backward* [from Judges]" (Jobling 1998: 33; emphasis in original). Concluding that the literary patterns of the book of Judges continue into 1 Samuel, and refusing to be tripped by the interruption that the book of Ruth (which points readers to David) inserts in the Christian Old Testament canons, Jobling's commentary on 1 Samuel starts (back) in the book of Judges. Jobling reads 1 Samuel backward, taking 1 Samuel as part of the "Extended Book of Judges," as well as forward (see also West 2019).

---

3. This is a common question for scholars who add more works on Jonah. T. A. Perry's excuse is that readers refuse to let go of preconceived readings plus "a failure of imagination to explore other literary and theological agendas" (Perry 2006: xiii).

4. I use the lowercase with my first person "i" out of respect to the other persons—"you," "she," "he," "it," "them" and "others"—without whom my "i" loses its subjectivity. I do not see the point in capitalizing my first person, for i exist because of and in relation to other persons and subjects.

5. "Commentary" is a specialized form of "reading," but commentary is not all there is to reading. While there are many examples of how the commentary business functions, there is yet to be an entry on it in the esteemed Society of Biblical Literature's *Bible Odyssey* (www.bibleodyssey.org, as of May 3, 2019).

1. Commentary Flows 3

The other inspiration for the forward-and-backward orientation of this commentary comes from the subversive indigenous wisdom of the late West Papuan artist Donatus S. Moulo Moiwend (aka Donet), who counts among the normal people (see Preface). Of critical relevance for this commentary is Donet's "roots and leaves" works, which subvert conventional thinking concerning the parts of a tree as metaphors for human generations. Conventional thinking takes the roots of a tree to represent the ancestors, the trunk to represent the parents and the branches to represent the current generation. The fruits and leaves, which are younger, delicate and in need of gentle care, represent the children. This logic is reflected in one of the teachings of Jesus: "I am the vine, you are the branches. Those who abide in me and I in them bear much fruit, because apart from me you can do nothing" (John 15.5, NRSV). Jesus represented the conventional thinking that the branches (current generation) cannot exist without the vine or tree-trunk (parents, teachers) and the roots (ancestors), and this complementary relation is necessary in order for the vine to bear fruits (read: next generation). Donet, giving expression to traditional Papuan wisdom, overturned this way of thinking in his body of works around roots and leaves.

For Donet, the leaves represent the ancestors because leaves give air for breathing and sap for healing (see Figure 1.1, on which Donet painted a face to represent the ancestors on a dried palm leaf). The leaves (ancestors) give the current generation life, sustenance and healing. The days of the ancestors have expired, but they are not absent from the world of the living. The ancestors continue to be present in the healing powers of (green) leaves, in the whispering and singing of leaves in the wind, and in the rattling of dry (brown) leaves when the wind blows them around or when living creatures step on them. According to Donet's way of thinking, the world of the ancestors is not separate from this world of the current generation. Rather, the people of the current time live in the world of the ancestors (compare to assumptions in traditional theology about world or city of God). This way of thinking may be unconventional to foreign minds, but it is deeply rooted and very traditional in Donet's Papua—the largest island in Pasifika (for the region of Pacific Islands, South Sea Islands, Oceania).[6]

The trunk (body) and the branches represent the current generation. They provide the base and veins for and from the leaves (ancestors), while the roots represent the children (future generation) because it is out of the roots that shoots (new life) spring. In Figure 1.2, the roots are also green to indicate that new life starts from the roots. Roots represent new beginnings and the life that wait in the future (read: next generation). Life comes out and up from the roots. Even when a new plant springs from dried seeds, the roots unfold first before the shoot rises.

Donet's thinking has support from two traditional corners: First, from an ancient literary culture, the "stump of Jesse" metaphor in the Bible proposes that "a branch from its roots will bear fruit" (Isa. 11.1). The tree is dead—a stump is

---

6. I use these designations interchangeably, depending on the argument that i make. Here, for instance, i use Pasifika to draw attention to native people and cultures. Below i use Oceania to draw attention to the oceanic context of the region.

Figure 1.1 Donatus S. Moulo Moiwend, *Guardian of the Palm Leaves* (oil on palm leaf, 2010). Used with permission of the Moiwend family.

what remains—but life is in the roots. And second, from ancient oral cultures, the mapping of *whakapapa* (Māori for genealogy) is commonly identified as "family tree" and because of the top-to-bottom reading orientation of most cultures the roots are taken to be the children and grandchildren (see Figure 1.3). The family tree grows down, and the future of life is underneath.

In honour of Donet, i turn the Jonah narrative over looking for roots at the end of the book, and so, following Jobling's lead, i read the narrative forward as well as backward. In reading Jonah both ways, the significance of the beasts and of the city of Nineveh (both of whom caught the focus in the final scene, Jon. 4.10-11) is taken seriously in this commentary. In reading backward (from the end to the beginning), one reads from the dusty, sandy and rocky hinterland of Nineveh, which invites one to *return* (to) the narrative with sand and pebbles in one's eyes and toes (a mark of islander criticism, see Davidson 2015).

Figure 1.2 Donatus S. Moulo Moiwend, *Tree of Life* (oil on bark, undated).[7] Used with permission of the Moiwend family.

The experience of paying attention to the agency of beasts while reading a narrative backward is similar to the experience of being sucked into the *moana* (deep sea) by a rip (see Havea 2007). A rip is like a washing machine: it spins and then wrings, and it may even bruise, its victim (in this context, the reader). One (i.e. a reader) cannot control a rip (a text), and one will drown if she or he fights back. One has a better chance of surviving by simply relaxing and allowing the rip to take her or him into the deep, then swim around the rip onto shore. Returning from the experience of drifting in a rip, familiar to islanders, to the

---

7. Responding to this artwork when i presented it at a meeting in Christchurch, New Zealand (October 2, 2018), Lavinia Latu shared these words with me: "The knowledge of our ancestors is like a green leaf full of life. We stand on the shoulders of our history like the branches of a tree, as its richness will bring life to the future of our generation."

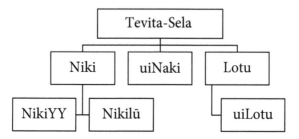

Figure 1.3 Family tree.

task of *commenting* on a biblical text, this EBC volume goes against the will of commentators who seek to determine and control texts and their meanings.

I did not flee from (but i did delay completing) this assignment, also, because i am not fully on board with the EBC agenda. There are aspects that i appreciate, like the six ecojustice principles—intrinsic worth, interconnectedness, voice, purpose, mutual custodianship, resistance (see Habel 2011: 1–2)—and the push for critical hermeneutics of suspicion, identification and retrieval (Habel 2011: 8–14), but i do not belong to the Western scholarly traditions that EBC challenges nor am i on board with the drift towards romanticizing the agency and voices of Earth[8] and of its creatures. I read for beasts, for instance, on land and in the sea, but i am mindful that i can only read as a native. Indigenous. Human. In other words, i have boarded the EBC boat because of its principles, but not because of its practices. Those principles are the starting points for this commentary. In other words, i assume but do not look for the ecojustice principles in the Jonah narrative.

So far, i have given the impression that i am an unruly runagate going for a ride on the EBC boat, away from the pride land (read: the commentary business) of biblical scholarship. And at some point, i will jump (fresh) off the EBC boat. At that point, notwithstanding, i will be grateful for the opportunity to also mark possibilities for the "radical re-orientation" of the EBC (as introduced in Habel 2011: 1–16). Key in my attempt at radical re-orientation is the appeal to the realities and imageries of natives of the sea and of (is)lands. Herein is one of the contributions of this EBC volume to the study of Jonah: analysing Jonah with native, sea and (is)land orientations (on islander criticism, see Havea, Aymer and Davidson 2015; Havea 2018b).

Hermeneutical rip

The hermeneutics of suspicion, identification and retrieval work well if they are stimulated to intersect, so that they are not three steps in a linear process but

---

8. "Earth" in this commentary "refers to the total ecosystem, the web of life, the domains of nature with which we are familiar, of which we are an integral part and in which we face the future" (Habel 2011: 3). In this ecosystem are inanimate objects as well, which have roles to play in the *web of life* and *domains of nature*.

that they become like curls in a rip. In this hermeneutical rip there needs to be a point of entry but one might end up at a different place than planned. Several scenarios are possible with the intersection of the three critical hermeneutics: suspicion could open the way for identification and retrieval, identification could set the tone for retrieval and suspicion, retrieval could require and at once invite identification and suspicion and so on. One may of course enter from two or more points bearing in mind, for instance, that suspicion against one subject may incite suspicion against other subjects, and the same applies in the case of identification and retrieval.

In the EBC hermeneutical rip, the objects of suspicion, identification and retrieval are many. For instance, hermeneutics of suspicion against anthropocentrism may be coupled with suspicion against dualistic views that see Earth as object for human interests, against linear ways of thinking, against the politics of identification, against the supremacism of retrieval missions and against Earth-centred mindsets that ignore the powers of Earth to reject, consume and subjugate. Earth is not impassive nor naïve. Hermeneutics of identification with the ways and place of non-human subjects and interests in biblical texts may also interweave with identification with the organic and inanimate bases of identification (so, for instance, one sees the sea, boat, shrub, worm, wind, city and beasts for who they are rather than as "non-humans"), with subjects who seem unable to escape suspicious and condemning eyes, and with disgusting subjects and repulsive texts that no one dares to retrieve. And hermeneutics of retrieval of the voices of Earth and minoritized members of the Earth communities may also seek the retrieval of subjects who have unjustly been under suspicion, of retrievable subjects whom rescuers abandon, and of victims of Earth and its communities.

God and the biblical narrator are also to be submitted to the hermeneutics of suspicion, identification and retrieval. A reading of the story of Jonah that does not critically engage with God and the narrator is not radical enough,[9] especially given that Jonah initially (Jonah 1) refused to follow God's direction and at the end (Jonah 4) he debated with God about his wish to die. In between, when Jonah finally went to Nineveh (Jonah 3), the narrator is not clear if he was sincere. Jonah did not say much when he landed on shore again. He (immediately?) walked for one day than he spoke four Hebrew words at Nineveh (Jon. 3.4), who responded immediately (Jon. 3.5-9), then he had his first spar of words with Yhwh (Jon. 4.1-4) before exiting to sulk from a place east of the city (Jon. 4.5). Initially Jonah did not commit to Yhwh's mission, and would have quietly exited if the narrator allowed him to die. It is tricky to be anthropocentric with this story because the key character wants to die, to stop being human, and the favoured subject is a great city with many people and animals. A great fish rescued the main character

---

9. In reading the narrative forward (see Chapters 2–3) and then backward (see Chapters 4–9), this commentary intentionally goes against the narrator's design.

8   *Jonah*

in the sea (Jon. 1.17),[10] and the repenting of beasts (Jon. 3.8-9) contributed to the sparing of the city and the people of Nineveh (Jon. 4.11). The Jonah narrative-and-novella, according to this overview, is far from being an anthropocentric construction.

There is no indication if the fish had a voice, and it could be forgiven for not saying anything because it had a foreign creature in its belly. Was the fish silent, or silenced? And did the fish hear the prayer of this human creature? On the other hand, the beasts in Nineveh are reported to have voices: they were among those that the king ordered to "cry mightily to God" (Jon. 3.7b-8a), and the beasts were heard by a relenting God. In the case of the beasts, the hermeneutics of retrieval is not required. Their voices are broadcasted in the text, already. Nonetheless, the hermeneutics of identification is needed with respect to the beasts (see Chapter 4) and the hermeneutics of suspicion need to ask—what prevents readers from hearing and identifying with beasts? Options for my line of queries will be spelled out in the following chapters.

The hermeneutics of retrieval, however, is needed to broadcast the voice of the city, Nineveh. The narrator describes Nineveh as wicked (Jon. 1.2) but also as "a large city of God, three days' walk across" (Jon. 3.3). Do the inhabitants, human and animal, represent the voice of the city? Could the voice of the city be more than the voice of its settlers? And could the voice of the city of Nineveh in the story of Jonah be different from that perceived in the history of biblical Israel? As one of the capitals of ancient Assyria, it is condemned (see Nahum) as representing the voice of destruction (see Gruber 2001). Nineveh, like Babylon, has been chanted down by many advocates of Israel.

It may seem strange to ask the above questions concerning a city qua an inanimate, human construction, given that this commentary is part of an ecological series and i am a native who is also a biblical critic trained in Western modes of interpretation. The strangeness of my questions is in part because of the popular assumption that native and indigenous peoples have nothing to do, and should not be concerned, with cities. We are supposed to be people of the wild(erness) and the bush, as compared to the civilized people who live in cities. I raise these questions, and will return to them later (especially in Chapter 6), for two reasons. First, to borrow the observation made by Habel, because "we are Earth beings,

---

10. Unless otherwise indicated, i follow the division of verses in the NRSV because that is the versification with which the majority of readers in the (English and) vernacular languages are familiar. I, however, do not always honour the NRSV structure, which conveys a particular reading of the narrative, and i structure the pericopes differently (here and there) based on the reading that i propose or reframe and the argument that i make. As expected in the commentary business, the meanings of a narrative change in relation to how it is structured, and there are many ways of structuring the Jonah narrative. Because of the oral and liquid contexts in which i live and read, in addition to the forward-and-backward orientations of this commentary, the structuring of the Jonah narrative is fluid (here and there).

not merely human beings. As such we are invited to read from the perspective of Earth, and *from within this habitat* called Earth" (Habel 2011: 16; my italics). Within this habitat called Earth, inanimate human constructions, like cities, contribute *loudly and mightily* to the conditioning of Earth. The construction and maintenance of cities, as well as the decisions and policies drawn in and funded by cities, affect the well-being of Earth, and so the *voices* of cities need to be engaged in an EBC volume. Second, i am concerned with inanimate objects because there are inanimate human constructions in Oceania that affect the conditions of our waters and (is)land space. A painful example is the Runit Dome constructed by the US military on Enewetak Atoll in the Marshall Islands, a crater over 350 feet deep into which radioactive waste from the testing of nuclear bombs in Enewetak and Bikini Atolls (1946–58) were dumped. With sea level rising, radioactive waste will spill into the ocean and devastate the seascape of the island community which was previously forced to move when the tests (estimated at 1.6 Hiroshima bombs each day, for twelve years) took place.[11] Time will tell the extent of the devastation caused by this US Dome, which locals call a Tomb. This human construction has a loud and mighty voice, but the world community does not see nor account for it.

My interest in reading for the voice of Nineveh is in order to hear the city itself, through its structures and its inhabitants, as well as to provide a platform for the interrogation of inanimate human constructions that are devastating Earth. This is part of the hermeneutical rip that the EBC series provides, and one of the contributions that this particular commentary makes to the study of Jonah. Put simply, the analysis of Jonah, and of other biblical books, can no longer be undertaken as if one is blind to and ignorant of the ecological injustices that surround us. The critique of academics by Filipino activist Emmanuel Garibay manifests my provocation (see Figure 1.4). *Akademiko* critiques academics who work for and appreciate the reward (represented by the apple) that they receive from their students and disciples but, when they remove their glasses, they cannot see the world in front of them. Their eyes are stuck to their reading glasses, and they are experts in reading texts but blind to the world in front of them. In this commentary, contexts do matter.

Contexts matter

The EBC series is intentional about analysing biblical texts in their literary and historical contexts, and with critical attention to the lived contexts of critics

---

11. Lesser known in the global community is the British Empire's moving (in 1950s and 1960s) of iKiribati natives to the Solomon Islands, where the second and third generations are beginning to wonder about the impact of atomic bomb testing on their "home" islands. They are spared that troublesome knowledge because they were not returned home, but they now have to raise their families on islands where they are out of place (by appearance, practice, culture and custom).

Figure 1.4 Emmanuel Garibay, *Akademiko* (oil on board, 2009). Used with permission of the artist.

and readers. With respect to the lived contexts, the EBC series encourages the foregrounding of two contextual dimensions: "Our environmental crisis and our ecological orientation" (Habel 2011: 3). Explicitly attending to these two dimensions makes the EBC series contextual, at the local and planetary levels. Because the contexts are lived, the environmental concerns are added to other matters of life and living. This is evident in Denis Edwards's critique, following upon Pope John Paul's call for ecological conversion, of the Christian church:

> Commitment to ecology has not yet taken its central place in Christian self-understanding. It is far from central in terms of its structure, personnel and money. As the church itself is called to conversion to the side of the poor in the struggle of justice and to the side of women in their struggle for full equality,

1. Commentary Flows

so the church itself is called to conversion to the side of suffering creation. (Edwards 2006: 3)

Accordingly, the EBC series joins the chorus of scholars for whom contexts and subjects that are marginalized matter in the commentary business.

But how biblical contextual interpretation is undertaken differs among biblical critics. Without entering the debate on whether and how all biblical interpreters and their interpretations are obviously contextual, suffice it to say here that biblical contextual interpretation is not done the same way by readers from the same context and that it is much more diverse in the global context.[12] At the risk of oversimplifying, i distinguish two general modes of conducting biblical contextual interpretation: first, some biblical critics analyse biblical texts from and for a specific context of living, past and/or present. What the text means in its literary and historical context sets the agenda for the contextual interpretation. How might the biblical text speak into a specific context? What does the text say for that context? In this mode, the biblical contextual interpreter appropriates the text into the context which, in the end, means appropriating the context for the sake of the text. The text is privileged, and the context is cast in the interest of the text. The prayerful Jonah in the belly of the fish (Jon. 2.1-9), for example— in contrast to the truant (Jon. 1.3), dormant (Jon. 1.5b) and angry (Jon. 4.1) Jonah—is taken as a model for people of faith. This contextual move is evident in the three theses on Jonah awarded by the Pacific Theological College: people of faith are to be compliant and prayerful, and to be unified (see Faʻaleava 1983), and the book of Jonah helps in opposing dissent and resistance. This proposal is sanctioned by the observation that God refused to give in to Jonah's rage (Jon. 4.4, 9a, 10-11). Moreover, emphasizing the so-called conversion of Nineveh in the Jonah narrative, people of faith are expected to be open to dialogue among themselves and with people of other faith traditions (see Nicole 1990; Wiliame 2017). The appropriation of the Jonah narrative by these three colleagues privilege the biblical text over the life world of Pasifika.

Given the EBC's commitments, the difficult task for this first mode of contextual interpretation is determining what, if anything, does Jonah say to the current ecological crisis. This requires an ecological conversion so that the moments of ecological crisis in the story (e.g. storm at sea, hot wind on land, death of a bush) are not read in the interest of humans only but in the interests of ecology in general (including fish, bush and worm) as well. Upon those observations, the critic determines what Jonah says to the current ecological crisis. As the narrator exercises authority in the narrative world, so do scholars operate in the commentary business.

---

12. This was evident in the opening plenary panel of the 2016 International Meeting of the Society of Biblical Literature (Seoul, South Korea). See a reflection on this panel in Havea and Lau (forthcoming).

The second mode of contextual biblical interpretation is where critics use something from a context (such as a saying, concept, theory, custom) to frame their analysis of a biblical text (e.g. the concept of *fara*, a Rotuman word that means "being relational or kinship," in Wiliame 2017). How might the context make sense of the biblical text? What in the text are (not) meaningful for the context? The historical setting of the text does not matter as much as the literary and ideological compositions of the text. The aim of the analysis in this second mode is not textual or cultural appropriation, but to engage and assess the content and baggage of the text. In the case of Jonah, how might the current ecological crisis frame and shape one's analysis of YHWH's change of heart concerning Nineveh? How do victims of some form of ecological crisis (e.g. cyclone, drought, tsunami, earthquake) cope with the sparing of the great city of Nineveh? There is room in this mode of biblical contextual interpretation for contesting the text.

I prefer the second mode of contextual biblical interpretation for the analysis of Jonah in this commentary, and i extend this critical mode of contextual interpretation to the (implicit) Western dimensions—in terms of both the Western heritage of biblical interpreters (see Habel 2001: 1, 8) and the Western legacy of biblical criticism (see Habel 2001: 9–10)—of the EBC series. What are seen to be ecological crises, and what are accepted as ecological orientations, differ from context to context, so Western and native critics will differ in our views, values, definitions and blind spots. I expect, and accept, differences. What is critical for me here are not the differences between my native perspectives and orientations[13] with those of Western critics, but what we overlook or cover over because of our contextual differences. In what ways have the attention to climate effect (as ecological crisis) in Tuvalu and Kiribati (intentionally?) covered over the ongoing devastations of the so-called Pacific War between the United States and Japan which was waged in the waters of Tuvalu and Kiribati (1942–5)? And how have debates about climate change and climate effect covered over the ecological crises caused by atomic testing conducted by the British, US and French governments in the waters of Oceania, from the Marshalls to Māʾohi Nui? These crises continue to traumatize the current generation of natives. The above questions shift the focus from ecological crisis and climate effect to climate (in)justice and the plights of victims of ecological and human-induced disasters. The latter relate to climate trauma. It is therefore not enough to shift one's contextual antennas from climate change to climate (in)justice when one reads biblical texts; it is also necessary to attend to the traces of climate trauma in biblical texts. Accounting for (read: swimming in) this hermeneutical rip is the ecological orientation that frames my analysis of Jonah in this commentary.

There is not much in this commentary that is neutral, or innocent. Or new (out of respect to developmental cultures) and original (out of respect to ancestral cultures). Rather, this commentary is contexted. Natively, it is framed by the realities of climate (in)justice and climate trauma. But the commentary is Jonah-

---

13. In spite of my Western(ized) training and career, i still read with native mindsets and biases. I am a self-confessing nativist in my orientation, but not in an essentialist manner.

like as well: it runs away from traditional and methodological expectations (read: the gods of the commentary business) and when it buys into the traditional expectations, it is not fully compliant.

Flowing both ways

Position and orientation matter in the spinning, writing, reading, telling, hearing and discussing of biblical texts. Who is where? On top. Over yonder. At the bottom. Down under. To the side. Overboard. What is (not) there? What is ignored? What is sidelined? To where are the stories oriented? From whom do they flee? Towards what? Stories are in motion. Movement. Flowing.

This commentary flows both ways, forward and backward. In the first part of the commentary, i offer ecological analyses that follow the flow of the narrative, with due respect to the omniscient narrator. I divide this short novella into two units, Jon. 1.1–2.10 and 3.1–4.11.[14] The call for ecological conversion frames my analysis of both units. With the first unit (Jon. 1.1–2.10), i take Jonah's prayer from the belly of the fish as a moment of conversion, and i analyse both the prayer (Jon. 2.2-9) and the preceding prose (Jon. 1.1–2.1) for openings towards ecological conversion (see Chapter 2). And with the second unit (Jon. 3.1–4.11), i take Yʜwʜ God's change of heart towards Nineveh as a moment of conversion also, and this provides the energy for the exchanges between Jonah and Yʜwʜ God in Jonah 3–4 (see Chapter 3). Chapters 2 and 3 make up the "Forward flow" of this commentary.

In the second part of the commentary i analyse Jonah backward, in six sections, beginning from the end of the narrative:

Jon. 4.10-11 (Chapter 4)
Jon. 4.1-9 (Chapter 5)
Jon. 3.1-10 (Chapter 6)
Jon. 1.17–2.10 (Chapter 7)
Jon. 1.4-16 (Chapter 8)
Jon. 1.1-3 (Chapter 9)

In reading the narrative backward, the novella opens up to ecological analysis (for the key subjects of Jon. 4.5-11 are a plant, a worm and a city with many humans and beasts) as well as to ecological hermeneutics for the voices of beasts and of the city of Nineveh. Whereas the first part of the commentary (forward flow) honoured the narrator's design, the second part (backward flow) flees from the presence of

---

14. The verses and chapters are distributed differently in the Hebrew Bible (MT and NJPS): Jonah 2 has eleven verses in the Hebrew Bible but ten verses in the NRSV (Jon. 2.1 in the Hebrew Bible is Jon. 1.17 in the NRSV). With the placement of this one verse (see discussion in Chapter 7), Jonah 1 has sixteen verses in the Hebrew Bible but seventeen verses in the NRSV.

the biblical narrator. It is in fleeing from the narrator's design and agenda that this commentary is especially radical, as the EBC series seeks to be.

There is however a degree of fraudulence in my double bi-textual flow and orientations, because the backward flow is drawn upon the forward flow of the narrative. I cannot read backward without first reading forward. I could of course stop with the forward flow, but i would miss out on seeing how the Jonah narrative opens up to non-traditional orientations and concerns. I would also miss out on being sucked into the hermeneutical rip that i have favourably, but with fear and trembling, described.

Methodologically, the forward flow of the commentary analyses the Jonah novella with the attention of narrative criticism to plot, character, tension and resolution. And the backward flow of the commentary focuses on the literary features of the various units, as is expected of a traditional commentary, but with ecological orientations. In both flows, there are something new and something old. And in both parts of the commentary, something intertextual weaves Jonah to other stories, both textual and oral, some historicized and some legendary.

There is no final, concluding chapter to this commentary. Instead, i invite readers to reflect on the difference that the double bi-textual flow, forward and backward, of this EBC volume could bring to the commentary business. Might it be time to reconsider whose voices and agendas are privileged in the commentary business, the hallowed ground of biblical studies? In addition to making sense of a biblical book in the current situation, with diverse orientations, crises and indulgences, might it help to also resituate (resettle, resit) biblical characters and motifs at discomforting and some strange places?

A mat for Jonah?

Jonah has a thick history of reception (see Sherwood 2000), but there has been no survey of the rejections of Jonah. This lack is telling given that "reception history" suggests that there is also "rejection history," and because the climate of rejection is stronger in the story of Jonah than the spirit of reception. Rejection opens (Jonah rejects YHWH God's mission) and closes (YHWH God rejects Jonah's wish to die) the story of Jonah. In between are several moments of rejection (in the form of change of mind, heart or ways, which are the substances of repentance and conversion): the city of Nineveh rejects its propensities towards wickedness, and YHWH God rejects an earlier decree to destroy Nineveh.

The interweaving of reception with rejection in the case of Jonah can be seen in local Pasifika communities. There are mixed feelings about this character: Jonah is reviled for bringing trouble to the boat and the sailors, but he is also revered for surviving the strains in the belly of the fish.[15] Parents who name a son after Jonah

---

15. Solomon Islands communities have similar legends which contemporary storytellers reframe to add that when the native was swallowed, he saw a message on the wall of the stomach of the fish—"Jonah was here."

hope that he will be *at one* with the sea (see Chapter 2)—a valued quality in the island settings. Those parents are not troubled by Jonah not being on the same page with YHWH God. The theological stresses in the relationship between Jonah and YHWH God do not overshadow the ecological feats of Jonah. But when trouble visits a family or community, the first question on the lips of the locals is *Ko hai 'oku Siona?* (Who is the Jonah?). In other words, who has brought the trouble on the family or community? Who is to be blamed? The premise here is that if that person is removed, the trouble will go away.

Responses to "Who is the Jonah?" vary. Some locals point at persons to blame; some raise their hands to accept the blame; some do not point or say anything and some simply laugh. Whatever the response may be, there is a shared belief that someone is responsible for the trouble that has befallen the family or community. In this regard, the troubling aspect of Jonah's character is embraced by local islanders. With regard to the ecological crisis, the world view of Pasifika natives allows for the blame to be accepted, shifted or mocked.

There is no solid and uncrossable barrier between the reception of Jonah and the rejection of Jonah, and between the revered Jonah and the reviled Jonah. These, to use a less challenging (compared to the rip) island image, are like strands in a weaving. The strands criss-cross to hold each other into place. When a strand slacks, slips or is missing, the tough strand stands and the weaving unravels. In this regard, the reception of Jonah is held into place by the rejection of Jonah, and the revered Jonah is meaningful in relation to the reviled Jonah.

Weaving creates many items, including hat, fan, basket and mat. The mat is a meaningful cultural artefact in Pasifika. It signifies welcome (see Tupou-Thomas 2004). When a guest(s) visits, the host rolls out a mat (if one is not already rolled out on the floor or ground) upon which they sit and visit through *talanoa* (story, telling, conversation).[16] If the woman or man of the house does not roll out a mat, she or he does not want or expect the guest to stay for long. They remain standing, in the open or at the door, have a quick chat, and the guest soon leaves. Without sitting on a mat, there is no opportunity for deep engagement or for building relationship. In light of the Pasifika mat custom, several elements in the Jonah narrative are open for reconsideration. What were the reasons for Jonah's rush through the great city of Nineveh? Jonah was in a hurry. He did not linger to greet or visit with the locals. And what are the implications of his not being invited into any of the local homes? Would he have accepted, and thus delay his journey, had he been invited?

When Jonah finally sat down under his booth (Jon. 4.5), to look over into the city to see what might happen to it, on what did he sit? This is a Pasifika type of

---

16. The word *talanoa* in some (but not all) Pasifika islands refers to three events: story, telling and conversation. This one word weaves together the story (*talanoa*), the (re)telling (*talanoa*) of the story and the conversations (*talanoa*) around the story and its (re)telling. In this regard one *talanoa* (story, telling, conversation) gives content and life to the other *talanoa* (story, telling, conversation). (For the nonnative "conversation analysis," see Person Jr. 1996: 15–30.)

question, for one usually sits on something (e.g. mat, leaves) so that one is protected from the dust and dirt of the ground. But also, one sits on something in order to protect the ground from one's sitting on it. In this regard, did Jonah protect the ground from his anger and grief (Jon. 4.1, 4.4)? The narrator gives attention to protecting Jonah from discomfort from above, with the coverings provided by the booth (Jon. 4.5) as well as by the plant (Jon. 4.6), but not with the discomfort to the ground. What difference would it make to one's ecological interpretation if Jonah is imagined to have sat on something, like a mat?

In Pasifika, a mat is needed for *talanoa* to take place deeply and meaningfully. For a story (*talanoa*) to survive it needs (re)telling (*talanoa*) and conversation (*talanoa*); for a (re)telling (*talanoa*) to have content and impact it needs story (*talanoa*) and conversation (*talanoa*); and for a conversation (*talanoa*) to have life it needs story (*talanoa*) and (re)telling (*talanoa*). And in the world of *talanoa*, a proverbial mat could be woven.

In the spirit of *talanoa*, this commentary weaves a mat not just for Jonah but also for the other earth(ed) characters in the narrative.

Part I

FLOWING FORWARD

Like the author of Job, he [the author of Jonah] chose an obscure figure from the past to be the main character in a theological tract that probes the nature of God's justice. His tactic, though, was to unhinge the audience's expectations by creating a wonderland in which a prophet tries to run away, foreigners act like Israelites, and the most wicked city imaginable repents on a massive scale. By destabilizing his hearers, possibly people whose rigid notion of divine justice had led them into self-righteous despair, the author prepared them to receive a radical message of God's compassion. (White 1992: 212)

Chapter 2

FLOW INTO THE SEA (JON. 1.1–2.10)

Taking Jon. 2.10 (when the fish "spewed Jonah onto dry land") as the end of the "Flow into the Sea" and the beginning of the "Flow into Nineveh," i read the first part of the narrative in three sections. The first section (Jon. 1.1-3) introduces the complication that sets the narrative in motion. YHWH ordered Jonah to go and deliver a message to Nineveh, and Jonah's response was to snub YHWH's service and flee to Tarshish instead. In boarding a boat, Jonah "flowed" the story into the sea. The second section (Jon. 1.4-16) narrates the big chase. YHWH hurled wind and fury upon the sea to interrupt Jonah's flight, and in response Jonah found a way to slip into the water. In the third section (Jon. 1.17–2.10), YHWH captured Jonah (with the help of a great fish) and held him for three days and three nights. Caught. That was supposed to be enough time for Jonah to calm down, and to *give in* to YHWH's service. Disciplined.

YHWH was the determined and controlling protagonist, and Jonah responded differently in the three sections. Jonah fled, got dunked and prayed. The exchanges between YHWH and Jonah unfolded in and around the energies, vessels, creatures and realities of the sea: boat, mariners, wind, water, fish, survival, journey, deliverance, wonder.

Jon. 1.1-3

> [1] The word of YHWH happened to Jonah son of Amittai saying, [2] "Arise, go to Nineveh, the great (גדל) city, and call against it, for their wickedness has come to face me." [3] Jonah arose to flee to Tarshish from the face of YHWH; he went down to Joppa and found a boat going to Tarshish, paid its fare and went down into it to go to Tarshish, away from the face of YHWH.

"Arise" (Jon. 1.2) is the first word from YHWH that happened (וַיְהִי in Jon. 1.1, lit. the word of YHWH "was") upon Jonah. This first word was in the form of a command: Get up! At that point, as he explained later (Jon. 4.2), Jonah was on his own "ground" (אדמה). The narrative does not name or locate where his ground was, but it did not have to be on the land of Canaan-Israel. Jonah's (home) ground could have been anywhere outside of Nineveh, and the use of "ground" brings to mind the garden story in which Yhwh made *ha'adam* (the person) out of the dust of *ha'adamah* (the ground; Gen. 2.7—see Berger 2016 for an Edenic reading of the garden story). Ha'adam was "dust of the ground" that became a "living being" when Yhwh blew "living breath" into its nostril. I see Jonah with a similar grounded make-up. He was a "ground(ed) being," and the words of Yhwh "happened" (upon him) in order to raise and move him. Arise. Go. Yhwh's words demand motion. Move. They aim to uproot Jonah from his ground and push him towards Nineveh. Be un-grounded. Jonah was to leave his home ground to become a foreigner, but his mission was not clearly (or necessarily) in and for the interests of the land of biblical Israel.[1] That Jonah might have been from Israel is not evident in this moving story, but many readers assume that this was the case. In this chapter, on the other hand, i break away from the uncritical assumption that Jonah was from and for biblical Israel. I flee from the interests of biblical Israel.

Towards the end of the book, Jonah finally sat down (Jon. 4.5). On that occasion, he was not commanded. He decided on his own to sit down, to be grounded. He sat down to see what will happen to the city (Jon. 4.6). There is no indication that, in sitting down, he was giving up. In other words, Jonah was not "standing down." Rather, in sitting down he positioned himself to engage and to be engaged. In between Yhwh's command (which uprooted him from his home ground) and Jonah's resolve to take a sitting grounded position, the narrative seesaws through several positions—up and down, dry and wet, blown and tossed, back and forth, in and out, swallowed and vomited out, condemned then spared and so on. The story is in motion. Flowing. Meandering. Crisscrossing. Weaving. Then, Jonah sat down. He became grounded again. Enough moving, for now. But the story did not stop there.

When Yhwh commanded Jonah "arise, go to Nineveh" (Jon. 1.2), the narrator did not locate Jonah's position (on the ground, as in Jon. 4.2) or how far he had to travel to enter Nineveh. He is introduced as a son of Amittai, which was most likely a later addition, thus locating him in the narrative of Israel (2 Kgs 14.25). He later identified himself as a Hebrew who "fears Yhwh, God of the heavens who made the sea and the dry land" (Jon. 1.9) but this awareness did not make him loyal to Yhwh. At that point, Jonah was fleeing from the face (presence) of Yhwh (Jon. 1.3b). He was a runagate. Moreover, being located in the narrative of Israel does not mean that he was committed to the land or the cause of Israel. He explained in Jon. 4.2 that he fled because Yhwh was "a compassionate and gracious God,[2] slow to anger, abounding in kindness, renouncing punishment," but Jonah

---

1. I draw a distinction between "historical Israel" (the Israel of historiography) and "biblical Israel" (the Israel that one finds portrayed in the biblical text). While i am interested in biblical Israel as a canonical entity, i do not confuse it with historical Israel or the modern State of Israel. Put another way, in the corridors of biblical studies it is helpful to bear in mind that "Israel" comes in three different forms.

2. In the shadows of the topic of God's compassion (see Timmer 2011; Youngblood 2013) are the topics of reconciliation (see De La Torre 2007) and forgiveness (see Bolin

did not say that he wanted Nineveh to be destroyed. Yнwн had issues with Nineveh, on account of their wickedness (Jon. 1.2), but Jonah at the beginning was not of the same mind as Yнwн. Even if Nineveh was a problem for Jonah, it did not have to be because of biblical Israel's interest (given that Nineveh was one of the capitals of Assyria, one of biblical Israel's arch-enemies). Jonah's strife was with Yнwн, for being quick to forgive and relent.

Jonah's response to the words of Yнwн was to rise and flee to Tarshish, thinking that this will take him away from the face of Yнwн (Jon. 1.3). While there are biblical references to Tarshish as a rich and wealthy coastal city (1 Kgs 10.22; Jer. 10.9; Ezek. 27.12; Ps. 72.10), there is no scholarly consensus as to its (physical) location and whether in the Jonah narrative it was a historical or a narrative (legendary) city. In this chapter, i take Tarshish as it is named, "a distant place." Jonah chose to go by boat, and he thereby oriented the story towards the sea (see also Vaka'uta 2014; Kunz-Lübcke (2016). He could have gone across on land, but i imagine him thinking that going by boat was an easier option. He could sit or lie down on the boat, and he would leave no footprints. Most importantly, he could lay-low in the boat and hide from the face of Yнwн during the journey. So he paid his fare, and "went down" into the boat (Jon. 1.3) all the way to its "innermost parts" (or womb; Jon. 1.5). Jonah arose from his home ground and oriented the story towards the sea, and in descending to the depth of the boat he "grounded" his position beneath the waterline. Into the boat, Jonah hid from roaming eyes. Into the sea, Jonah floated away from the firm ground of dry land.

Yнwн commanded Jonah to rise and go to a recognized city, Nineveh "the great (גדל) city"; Jonah instead went into the sea, towards a legendary distant land. On a first reading, fleeing into the sea does not appear to be for the purpose of escaping from Yнwн. Jonah later acknowledged that Yнwн made the sea (Jon. 1.9), and he therefore would have assumed that the domain of the sea was under the sovereignty of Yнwн. According to this first reading, in fleeing into the sea Jonah descended into Yнwн's deeper lair. Why would he go there, if he was trying to escape Yhwh? On a second reading, when Jonah departed from the ancient seaport city of Joppa in the Mediterranean Sea, he headed away from the eyes of Yнwн which were turned towards Nineveh (further inland, by the Tigris River). If Jonah was to continue on his sea path, he would be far away from Nineveh. Assuming that Yнwн was watching Nineveh, as Jonah himself does later in the narrative (Jon. 4.5), the further away Jonah was from Nineveh the further he would get away from the face (presence) of Yнwн. In this second reading, the sea was an option for a quick and clear breakaway. The sea is not just a route, but a hideaway place as well. Tarshish was far away, literally a "distant land," but the sea was for now Jonah's place of refuge.

1997; Gaines 2003). I do not dwell on the topics of reconciliation and forgiveness in this study, but the resources noted above are helpful points of entry to those topics in relation to the Jonah narrative.

Jonah's flight took two steps, over two terrains. First, over land, when he arose and departed from his home ground. And second, into the sea, when he boarded the boat at Joppa. He started to flee to Tarshish before he reached Joppa (Jon. 1.3a), but the narrative does not explain how far he journeyed from his home ground to reach Joppa. It would have been far enough to tire him out, for he went into the boat and went to sleep (Jon. 1.5). The narrative also does not explain if crossing the sea was part of his original plan or it came up as an alternative to crossing on land. For a person seeking refuge, the sea is easier (if one could afford to pay the fare) and quicker. But it is also costly and dangerous for landed people. At Joppa, Jonah joined other travellers to Tarshish (Jon. 1.3b). His companions were not fleeing from Yhwh's presence, but they will also be affected in what happen—the good, the bad and the ugly—at sea. For the other travellers, the sea was not fearsome or cause for panic. On the other hand, the sea was an artery through which they could reach a distant land. They too must have paid their fare, and had courage to put their lives in the hands of the mariners. Clearly, there is no fear of the sea in this first section. Readers who imagine fear of the sea in this narrative see more than the text reveals.

Ecological flow

The narrative crosses over and into several *places*, five of which are presumed and two are anticipated. The five presumed places are the domain from where Yhwh spoke (which could be over or on land, close to where Jonah was), the home ground where the word of Yhwh *happened* to Jonah and from where he arose to flee, the port area of Joppa, the inside of the boat and the sea. These places are presumed but not all are presented or described for the reader, and the port and the boat link the land to the sea. The two anticipated places are Nineveh (which is reached later) and Tarshish (which is named but never reached, and so it remained an ideological place). In the opening three verses, the narrative materializes and intersects these seven places, with a land-and-sea link.

The narrative invites readers to anticipate punishment against Nineveh (on the basis of Jon. 1.2), and in the next verse the narrative connects the land to the sea (Jon. 1.3). Given that the flow of the narrative is towards the sea, one wonders if the consequence of Nineveh's wickedness will also flow into the sea. But Yhwh disconnected Nineveh from both the land and the sea by presenting it as "that great city." The anticipated Nineveh was a constructed place, a city. Moreover, Yhwh presented the city as an agent that is responsible for the wickedness (of its inhabitants) which has "come up" before him (Jon. 1.2). This could be taken as a hint that the city has a voice, but the city is not free(d) from the voices of its inhabitants. To retrieve the land from Yhwh's demeaning judgement invites seeing the anticipated punishment of the city (which needs to be retrieved from the shadows of its inhabitants) as a burden upon the land, which in Jon. 1.2 flows into the sea.

Yhwh and the narrator do not consider whether the land and the sea have voices of their own. They are *hidden places* in this section of the narrative—the sea

2. Flow into the Sea

is hidden under the port and the boat, and the land is hidden under the city—but their connection enabled Jonah to temporary flee from the presence of YHWH. Jonah fled on land first, then he went into the sea. Jonah may have escaped the eyes of YHWH, but not from the eyes (face, presence) of the land and the sea. In the same vein, the anticipated punishment of Nineveh will not be able to escape the eyes of the land and the sea. In this connection, the land and the sea are *omniscient places* in this narrative.

Jon. 1.4-16

[4] Then YHWH hurled a great (גדל) wind into the sea, and there was a great storm in the sea, that the boat thought of breaking up. [5] The mariners were afraid, and each cried to his God, and they cast the baggage that were in the boat into the sea, to lighten it for them. Jonah had gone down to the belly of the boat, laid down, and was fast asleep. [6] The captain came to him, and said to him, "What have I here, a sleeper. Arise, call to your God, perhaps God will think upon us and we do not perish."

[7] Meanwhile, they said each one to his fellow, "Come, let us cast lots so that we may know who caused this evil upon us." They cast lots, and the lot fell upon Jonah. [8] They said to him, "Tell us please, for whose cause is this evil upon us: what is your work, from where have you come, what is your country (ארץ), and from what people are you?" [9] And he said to them, "I am a Hebrew. I fear YHWH, God of the sky, who made the sea and the dry land." [10] And the men were greatly (גדל) afraid, and they said to him, "What is this that you have done?" For the men knew that he fled from the face of YHWH, because he had told them. [11] And they said to him, "What shall we do for you, so that the sea may calm from upon us?" since the sea was going and storming. [12] He said, "Pick me up and cast me into the sea, and the sea shall calm against you, for I know that it is because of me that this great storm is upon you." [13] Nevertheless, the men rowed to return to dry land; but they couldn't, because the sea was going and storming. [14] They cried to YHWH, and they said, "Oh YHWH, do not let us perish because of this man's life (נפש), and do not lay upon us innocent blood, for you YHWH have done as you pleased." [15] Then they picked Jonah up, cast him into the sea, and the sea stood from its raging. [16] The men thus feared YHWH with a great fear; they sacrificed a sacrifice to YHWH, and they vowed vows.

The sea is more than a place. The sea in itself was not the problem. The boat set off from Joppa, and the sea was calm about it. The sea became a problem when YHWH came casting and hurling his powers upon the sea. Things are not as expected. Against the expectation of the natives of the sea that a great storm is caused by the sea itself gathering its energy and brewing up a storm with fury, the narrative attributes the troubling of the sea to YHWH. YHWH was clearly not in a good mood. Looking like a big bully at a school yard, YHWH threw wind and fury "upon the sea" causing the boat to think about breaking up (Jon. 1.4). In trouble, the boat thought of a response (see Chapter 8). There is disconnection and unreasonableness in the bullying acts of YHWH. Jonah was the problem for YHWH, and the sea gets blown and tossed as a result. The sea became the target for no fault of its own, and the boat was traumatized.

Readers who have no physical connections with the sea, or who do not realize the many connections between living on dry land and the energies and resources of the sea, may not be troubled by the acts of YHWH. Those readers might see the sea simply as a highway and a dumping ground, and i would understand their indifference given their distance from the sea. But i imagine that those readers would still be troubled by images and stories of the floating plastic islands in the Pacific Ocean, or of the concrete US domes (e.g. the tombs at Runit, Marshall Islands) that are leaking radioactive waste into the seas of Micronesia. Readers do not have to be people of the sea to see the problem with those situations, and they do not have to accept the scientific arguments for global warming to find the rising sea level problematic for low-lying coastlines and islands. Plastic and nuclear waste have been hurled into the sea, and they and warmer than usual temperatures cause havoc among people for whom the sea is both their home and the main ground of resources for their living and thinking (so Vaka'uta 2014). I expect readers who are troubled by these modern realities to also find problems with the troubling of the sea by YHWH in the story of Jonah. Those readers might also be troubled with YHWH using the energies of nature (e.g. wind) for personal vendetta, notwithstanding that YHWH is believed to have made the earth and the sea. It is expected of a creator to protect and nurture the creation, rather than to do whatever it pleases with the creation. In this connection, YHWH acts without consideration.

The boat, on the other hand, is presented as having the capacity to consider: "The boat thought about breaking" (Jon. 1.4b). It was not a mindless vessel. This is an important portrayal to note in an EBC project, because "earth" contains both breathing creatures and inanimate subjects. And the inanimate subjects (boat, city) in the story of Jonah are not duds. The boat could think, and the great city of Nineveh, in the eyes of YHWH, could act (albeit wickedly; Jon. 1.1). Juxtaposing Nineveh's alleged wicked actions with YHWH's casting of wind and storm upon the sea makes me wonder what else was in the mind of the boat. If the boat thought that YHWH was (as) wicked (as Nineveh), i would understand. In this reading, the boat (like Jonah) was not of the same mind as YHWH. This begs the question of whether the narrator was of the same mind as YHWH or was hiding behind the characters of Jonah and the boat to expose and problematize views concerning YHWH. Going back to the world of *talanoa*, in which storytellers are not mindless or innocent, i imagine that this narrator too "thought about breaking" something.

The mariners were afraid and they cried each to his God,[3] then they threw the cargo overboard (Jon. 1.5). The reason for their fear is not identified. As workers

---

3. I capitalize "God" here because i do not agree that the deities of non-Hebrews are lesser beings in comparison to the *'elohim* of the Hebrews and Christians.

over the sea, they would be familiar with the impact of wind and storms. No sailor expects smooth sailing, or the sea to be calm with every voyage. There must have been something in this storm that frightened them, and throwing the cargo overboard benefited the boat. The sailors must have thought that the boat might break up, so they were of the same mind as the boat. The sailors were God-fearers (so Chen 2004: 293), and they, like many others, called on their God when they are in trouble. I imagine that the captain also called on his God before he cried to Jonah: "What is this, that you sleep soundly? Arise, call upon your God. Perhaps God will think of us, and we do not perish" (Jon. 1.6). During times of trouble, passengers too are called upon to do something in order to help secure the boat.

Jonah went into the belly of the boat, laid down and had fallen asleep (Jon. 1.5b). He found rest, even as the boat was tossed and twirled upon the waves. A secured soul could sleep in such a situation, or someone who was extremely tired. I imagine that Jonah must have been very tired when he boarded the boat. His tiredness would be in part because of how far and how quickly he travelled from his home ground to Joppa. When the captain woke him up, there is a clear tone of disbelief: how could he sleep so soundly! There is no hint of accusation or blame. Rather, the captain called for solidarity. He called Jonah to rise up and add his prayer to the prayers of the others. In this reading, the captain and the sailors were concerned for the safety of the boat and of everyone on board. That (compared to gaining wages) was the main objective of their job, and on this occasion, they asked for help from Jonah and the other travellers. But Jonah did not respond to the captain. Jonah did not say or do anything. Was he too tired to wake up to the captain's bidding? Assuming that the baggage thrown overboard was taken out of the "belly of the boat," Jonah would have slept through the commotion of the crew emptying out the boat as well as the captain's wake-up call.

The blame game (which humans are good at, going back to the garden story in Genesis 2–3) started when "each man to his fellow" casted lots to determine "for whose cause this evil" was upon them (Jon. 1.7). While the captain and the sailors are not excluded from this group of men, the other male travellers are drawn into readers' attention. There must have been women and children among the travellers, but the narrative does not include them in the blame game. The casting of lot here was men's business. And the lot fell on Jonah. So they asked Jonah for four pieces of information that would explain if he has caused evil upon them: his work (occupation, business), where he comes from (his home ground), his country (or land; ארץ) and his people (Jon. 1.8). The men seem curious that Jonah might be a crook or involved in a forbidden profession; that he might hail from an evil home, a son of a no-good or empty parent(s); that he might belong to a godforsaken country; or that his people might hereditarily be wicked. These are among the markers of "evil people" which have motivated stereotypes and fuelled expressions and acts of discrimination, the extreme cases of which are apartheid and genocide, with the holocaust of the Jews in Europe and the massacre of Tutsis in Rwanda as bloody examples. Closer to home for me is the ongoing genocide of West Papuans whose mineral rich land has been occupied by Indonesia since the early 1960s (see MacLeod 2015; Haluk 2017).[4] Jews and Tutsis were denoted for extermination because supremacist overlords took them to be cockroaches (worse than "evil people"), and this is ongoing in the case of the native West Papuans.

Jonah's response was brief and cheeky: "I am a Hebrew. Yhwh, the God of heaven—the one who made the sea and the dry land—I fear (ירא)" (Jon. 1.9). Jonah made no reference to his occupation or country, but he located himself with a people and their God. In response, the men were exceedingly afraid (note that ירא is repeated and heightened with גדל in Jon. 1.10a: האנשים יראה גדולה וירא). The fear of the men was more intense than Jonah's. They pushed Jonah, and he accepted responsibility: it was because he was fleeing from his fearsome God (Jon. 1.10b) that the storm has come. And he proposed a solution: that they cast him into the sea, and the sea will calm down (Jon. 1.12). The men did not accept his proposal, and instead rowed hard towards dry land. But the sea became more tempestuous against them (Jon. 1.13). They cried to Yhwh to not let them perish on account of Jonah and to not lay upon them "innocent blood" (Jon. 1.14). Then they took Jonah, cast him into the sea, and the sea responded by standing back from its raging (Jon. 1.15). In light of the "flow into the sea" orientation of this chapter, five details in this section stand out.

First, the narrative attributes the agitating of the sea to Yhwh but accredits Jonah for calming the sea down. Yhwh did not appear to have a clear plan—the men even accused Yhwh of acting as he pleases (Jon. 1.14b)—other than to trouble the sea in order to get at Jonah. But Jonah was not alone in the sea. Yhwh was not mindful of other subjects who were also affected by his troubling of the sea, including the sea itself. Jonah's solution put his flight on hold. He was no longer focused on himself or on Yhwh. His proposed solution was out of concern for (suggesting that he was of the same mind as) the boat, the crew and his fellow travellers. This is the obvious explanation for his proposal, except that these subjects are not named in the solution that he proposed: "Pick me up and cast me into the sea, and *the sea shall calm against you*, for I know that it is because of me that this great storm is upon you" (Jon. 1.2; my italics). Jonah named the sea, and his goal was to calm (שתק) it down. The sea did not deserve the "raging" (Jon. 1.15) that it was enduring, and Jonah calmed down both the body and the voice (taking שתק as "to quieten down") of the sea. Jonah did not present his proposal as part of a combat against Yhwh; but even if the events at sea are read as a contest between Jonah and Yhwh, Jonah clearly had the upper hand. The sea responded to Jonah. As a consequence, Jonah (with his body) released Yhwh's control from over the sea. Jonah helped the sea return to the stage in which it was when he stepped into the boat—the sea became calm—as well as brought calmness to the boat, the crew and the other passengers.

Second, the body of Jonah was thrown into the sea not as payment but as remedy. Jonah was thrown into the sea not in order that the men might receive

---

4. The United Liberation Movement for West Papua (ULMWP) maintains a website with updates on the "hidden" genocide and the fight of West Papuans for self-determination and independence (see www.freewestpapua.org).

some reward in return, but in order that the sea may calm down from its raging. The focus and emphasis is on the sea. Of course, a calm sea was of benefit to the travellers. But the drive of this reading is to emphasize that Jonah's body was offered as a cure for the sea from the "terrible storm" that was troubling it thanks to YHWH. The ailment of the sea was on account of Jonah, and he was the cure. The body of Jonah was both poison and remedy, a "gift" in the bilingual senses of the word (English "present" and German "poison"). In this "flow into the sea" reading, the gift in and of the body of Jonah to provide remedy is significant. The body of Jonah was the remedy for the sea in this section, and for the city of Nineveh in the next part of the narrative (see Chapter 3). This reading affirms the questions that Mariana Waqa raises in her poem "Paradise" (2019, used here with her permission):

> have you ever seen the ocean kneel?
> soften its waves at a command?
> Moses might have parted the Red Sea
> but our ancestors swallowed the oceans whole.[5]

Waqa expects the sea to listen to but not necessarily to obey a voice, and she leaves room for the possibility that the sea could accept a gift (especially from descendants of "ancestors who swallowed the oceans whole").

Third, Jonah could have jumped on his own into the sea and thus spared the men from the trauma of throwing him overboard. On the other hand, Jonah's direction that the men take him up and throw him overboard made them participate in the calming of the sea. This was not a one-man show, but a collaboration between Jonah and men who were strangers to him. The body of Jonah became the men's first gift, offered to the sea, before they offered a sacrifice to YHWH (in Jon. 1.16) after the storm. In this regard, the sea received the recognition and respect of Jonah and the men first. This is not an argument for the sea as divine. It is not necessary for the sea, or for anything, to be divine in order to receive a gift or sacrifice. One could offer a gift or sacrifice to any idol or to a homeless person, in the same way that these men offered Jonah as a gift to the sea. Receiving a gift is not a privilege only for divine beings. By being presented with a gift, the men recognized and appreciated the sea. But this is not to say that the sea thereby was more special than other subjects who receive gifts.

Fourth, when the men offered their gift, they referred to Jonah as "innocent blood." The depth of their distress could be heard in their cry to YHWH: "Do not let us perish by the life of this man, and do not put upon us innocent blood" (Jon. 1.14). They were seeking pardon from YHWH, for they were about to throw a man who claimed to fear YHWH overboard (Jon. 1.9). YHWH was not the God that they worshipped (cf. Jon. 1.5), and their seeking absolution from YHWH did not necessarily mean that they recognized YHWH as God. This was not a conversion story. Rather,

---

5. Waqa here echoes lines attributed to Warsan Shire: "You think I'll be the dark sky so you can be the star? I'll swallow you whole."

the men acknowledged that they were gifting the sea with a body that did not belong to them or to their Gods. It was out of respect, rather than in allegiance.

Fifth, the impact of the men's action on themselves was that they "feared YHWH with a great fear, they sacrificed a sacrifice to YHWH, and they vowed vows" (Jon. 1.16). The korban that the men sacrificed and the commitments that they vowed are not revealed.[6] The narrative spares those details, but emphasizes the fear of the men: they "feared a great fear." Earlier, the men "feared a great fear" (Jon. 1.10a) when Jonah revealed that he was a Hebrew who feared YHWH. Their fear at that point was not directed at YHWH. At the closing of this section, the narrator explains that the object of their great fear was YHWH. This time, they complemented their fear with a sacrifice and vows. Did these men become worshippers of YHWH, as the majority of commenters conclude? This is not the only way to read their great fear, sacrifice and vows. I take my cue from Jonah, who feared but did not obey YHWH. Even as he was fleeing from the face of YHWH, he still declared that he feared YHWH (Jon. 1.9). In the case of Jonah, fear does not lead to obedience or worship. So there are two possible conclusions here: first, that one could fear (read: worship) without fully agreeing and accepting YHWH (the case of Jonah) and second, that one could fear without worshipping YHWH (the case of the men).

Ecological flow

Reading "into the sea," the reading proposed here invites both sympathies towards Jonah and suspicions against YHWH. This reading releases Jonah from the land and interests of (ancient, biblical, modern) Israel, and exposes the absurdity of YHWH's response to Jonah's flight. In the case of Jonah, YHWH does not recognize freedom to (not) adhere. In this reading also, the subjectivity of the sea, the boat, the mariners and the passengers are recognized and engaged. They are characters with mind, will and ability, and they do not have to serve the interests of YHWH or the narrator. Jonah oriented the story into the sea, and the men on board dunked his body as a gift in the interest of the welfare of the sea. Then the men offered a sacrifice with vows, as if to help calm YHWH down. The sea stood back from raging, thanks to Jonah; YHWH gave up the chase, thanks to the men on board.

For boat travellers in Pasifika, an important element is missing from the narrative. Jonah did not take, and none of his fellow travellers offered to share, a "boat bed" (*mohenga vaka*) with him on board.[7] This is usually a small mat that one would roll out to sit and lie on during the journey, for our local boats do not have cabins with beds, sheets and blankets like the modern ferries in Western countries, and it is a sign of destitution when someone sits or lies on the bare, naked floor. Travellers spread out on deck, and would be sympathetic with Jonah

---

6. Without these details, insofar as the narrative is concerned, the sacrifice and vows are empty. They are made, but they have no content.

7. This kind of detail is important to Pasifika storytellers, compared to the biblical narrator's attention to the details of prayer, sacrifice and vows.

that the biblical narrator did not give him a mat (boat bed). How might a mat be provided for Jonah? The understanding and sympathetic reading provided here serve as a proverbial mat upon which Jonah might sit and rest. The collaboration between Jonah and the men calmed the sea, a gift desperately needed in the present-day contexts of sea level rising with more frequent and stronger cyclones. In the interest of the sea, a Jonah-like solution would be helpful at this time also. Hence the loaded question of Pasifika natives is still relevant, "Who is the Jonah" (see Chapter 1) in the current time?

Jon. 1.17–2.10

1.17 And Yhwh provided a huge fish to swallow Jonah
And Jonah was in the gut of the fish for three days and three nights
2.1 And then Jonah prayed to Yhwh his God from the gut of the fish
2 And he said
    I called from my trouble to Yhwh
    And he answered me
    From the belly of Sheol I cried
    And you heard my voice
    3 You cast me into the depth
    Into the heart of the sea
    The flood surrounded me
    Your breakers and billows swept over me
    4 And I said, I am cast from before your eyes
    Yet I will gaze again to your holy temple
    5 The waters closed on me, even to the soul
    The deep surrounded me
    Weeds tangled to my head
    6 I sank to the base of the mountains
    The bars of earth shut upon me for good
    Yet you raised my life from the pit
    Yhwh, my God
    7 When my soul fainted against me
    I remembered Yhwh
    And my prayer came into you
    To your holy temple
    8 The ones who heed lying breaths
    Forsake their own mercy
    9 But I, with voice of thanksgiving
    Will sacrifice to you
    What I vowed, I will appease
    Deliverance for Yhwh
10 Then Yhwh spoke to the fish
And it vomited Jonah onto dry land.

YHWH changed his approach, converted from chasing Jonah to rescuing him instead. But it was a strange rescue because, instead of pulling Jonah up for air, YHWH provided a great fish to swallow and drag him deeper into the sea; and Jonah was in the belly of the fish for three days and three nights (Jon. 1.17). YHWH's rescue process is difficult to comprehend, but the plot is believable: a man who could sleep soundly in the middle of a storm would have no trouble reclining in the gut of a fish.[8] In the world of *talanoa*, the "ride" in the gut of the fish would be believable. With no room to move, Jonah was silent for three days and three nights. Trapped. Not that time matters in the belly of a fish, but it took Jonah that long to come to a mind of prayer. The 1–conjunction ("then") at the beginning of Jon. 2.1 suggests that Jonah started to pray after the three days and three nights. He could no longer flee, and then he came to YHWH in prayer. In this connection, Jonah's prayer was not out of desperation, as if he was dying to exit from the fish. Having rested, Jonah reached the state of prayerfulness.

In the face of trouble, Jonah was a "cool" (calm and collected) character. He did not have any hang-ups about his running away from the face of YHWH. He did not feel guilty about not being of the same mind as YHWH. When pushed, he openly (and proudly?) explained that he was running away from YHWH (Jon. 1.10). This was not a problem for the narrator, for whom there was no doubt that Jonah understood YHWH as his God (Jon. 1.9, 2.1). There is no reason in the narrative to assume that Jonah's running away should be read as rejection of YHWH. Jonah expected YHWH his God to be located in particular places (e.g. the holy temple in Jon. 2.4 and 2.7), and he did not expect YHWH to have sovereignty over other places (e.g. the distant land Tarshish and in the sea). YHWH his God was not a universal sovereign. There were many Gods in the story world of Jonah, and both Jonah and the narrator were cool with this detail also.

Jonah was cool enough that he would have slept through the storm if the captain had not woken him, and he was peaceable in the gut of the fish for an extended stretch of time. Three days and three nights! So when he prayed from the gut of the fish, i do not see him as one who was desperate or contrite. He kept his cool, and in the prayer he had another "run" ("dash" or "go") at YHWH his God. I read the prayer in two parts out of respect to the differentiation that Jonah made between his call (קרא) and cry (שׁוע) to YHWH (Jon. 2.2-6) and his prayer (תפלה) to YHWH (Jon. 2.7-9). The two parts (alternative translation is provided below) have different drives and concerns.

[2] And he said,
I called from my oppression to YHWH, and it answered me
From the belly of She'ol I cried, and you heard my voice
[3] For you casted me into the deep

---

8. While the plot is believable in relation to the events narrated in the previous chapter, the story is not. Moreover, being believable in the narrative world does not mean that the plot and the story are possible. Believability and possibility are not the same.

Into the heart of the seas
And the floods surrounded me
All your waves and billows broke over me
⁴ And I said, I am cast out of your eyes
Until I will again gaze upon your holy temple
⁵ The waters flowed over my life
The deep surrounded me
Weeds wrapped about my head
⁶ I sank to the base of the mountains
The earth with its bars closed upon me
But you raised my life from the pit
Yʜᴡʜ my God. (Jon. 2.2-6)

The opening words could be read in two ways: first, that out of his oppression he called to Yʜᴡʜ, and second, that he called from out of his oppression-to-Yʜᴡʜ (אל־יהוה). The first option is the popular understanding, which presents Yʜᴡʜ as the deliverer (see Jon. 2.9) who heard and responded to Jonah's distress call. The second option follows the MT word order and attributes Jonah's oppression (צרה) to Yʜᴡʜ. Jonah was in trouble, and Yʜᴡʜ was his troubler. When both options are taken together, Yʜᴡʜ is the problem as well as the solution, the oppressor as well as the deliverer, the poison as well as the therapy, in other words, Yʜᴡʜ was the "gift" for Jonah.

Jonah was grateful that Yʜᴡʜ heard his voice when he cried from the belly of Sheol (Jon. 2.2), but that did not, as a result, stop him from exposing Yʜᴡʜ as his oppressor. Jonah's accusation is very critical in native islander eyes. The men threw Jonah into *the sea*, but Jonah accused Yʜᴡʜ of throwing him into *the deep*, into the heart of the seas, where floods, waves and billows broke upon him (Jon. 2.3), waters covered his life, (sea)weed wrapped his head (Jon. 2.5), the earth closed from him, and he sank to the bottom of the (sea)mountains (Jon. 2.6a). This overview distinguishes *the sea* from *the deep* (תהום) and draws on Gen. 1.1-2 and the layering of the universe as sky, earth (including dry land and sea; cf. Gen. 1.9-10) and the deep (תהום, which is presented as the realm of darkness). Jonah sank to the bottom of the deep; his oppression was severe, and Jonah attributed all of those to Yʜᴡʜ his God.

Jonah's call (קרא) and cry (שוע) did not convey belief or loyalty. In this reading, on the other hand, Jonah's call and cry indicted Yʜᴡʜ. In other words, Jonah took another "dash" at Yʜᴡʜ. Yʜᴡʜ was responsible and had to respond, not because Yʜᴡʜ was Jonah's God but because Yʜᴡʜ was Jonah's oppressor. Yʜᴡʜ could have ignored Jonah, but he instead heard him and pulled him out of the pit. The type of call and cry that Jonah uttered do have a place in the world of prayer. And there is also a place for words of commitment and comfort in the world of prayer, as in the second half of Jonah's prayer (Jon. 2.7-9).

⁷ When my life ebbed against me
I remembered Yʜᴡʜ
And my prayer came into you

Into your holy temple
[8] The keepers of empty silliness
Forsake their own interest
[9] But with voice of thanksgiving, I will sacrifice to you
What I have vowed, I will fulfill
Salvation is for Yhwh. (Jon. 2.7-9)

Jonah's prayer (תפלה) came when he remembered Yhwh, and he accredited this awareness to his realization that his life (נפש) was ebbing against him (Jon. 2.7). In this reading, Jonah's life was tormenting him rather than fainting away as in the NJPS rendering, "When my life was ebbing away." In the face of torment, Jonah remained cool. His prayer (תפלה) was not for the purpose of securing deliverance or comfort for himself, but simply because he remembered Yhwh. Nothing dramatic is presumed here, other than the evidence that Jonah had temporarily forgotten Yhwh. But now that he has remembered Yhwh, he committed to offer sacrifice with thanksgiving and to fulfil the vow he has made (Jon. 2.9). Compared to the "keepers of empty silliness [who] forsake their own interest," Jonah is committed to find salvation "for Yhwh" (ליהוה; 2.9c). The sacrifice he will offer and the vow he will fulfil are in the interest of Yhwh: "Salvation is for Yhwh." In this regard, Jonah committed to be Yhwh's deliverer.

The first half (call) focuses on Jonah, while the second half (prayer) focuses on Yhwh. The first half affirms the deliverance of Jonah by Yhwh, while the second half affirms that Jonah will find salvation for Yhwh. Both the critical voice in the first half and the comforting voice in the second half belong in the world of prayer.

Ecological flow

The two parts of this section unfold in different places and flow with different orientations. The call and cry (first part) came from the belly of She'ol, from the deep at the heart of the sea,[9] but it does not name to whom it was directed. Like an SOS call, it was made to whoever was out there on that wavelength. Jonah's cry and call came "out of the depth," an expression that scholars associate with biblical laments.[10] Yhwh responded to Jonah's cry and call, and Jonah was grateful.

On the other hand, the prayer (second part) was unambiguous: it was directed at Yhwh, and it located Yhwh at a constructed location, the holy temple. I take both the natural (albeit mythological) world of the cry and call and the constructed world of the prayer as earth(ed) places in Jonah 2. Earth is more than the so-called natural world; earth also includes constructed places like the temple (holy or

9. I take She'ol, *the deep* and the *heart of the sea* as referring to the same unknown and unreachable place. These are registers that help one imagine a place, but they do not locate that (mythological) place in space and time.

10. In the Solomon Islands, "out of the depth" is the literal meaning of the name "Lauru" which is the native name of the island that European colonialists renamed as Choiseul.

otherwise). The flow from call and cry into prayer suggests that the natural and the constructed (earthed or naturalized) also interflow. This possibility invites one to imagine that the happenings in and of the temple broke over and engulfed Yhwh (similar to how waves and billows broke over Jonah), and that the physical and ideological "bars" of the temple closed upon Yhwh. Yhwh struggled with the temple as Jonah did with the elements of the deep, and Jonah's prayer, sacrifice and vow facilitated the deliverance of Yhwh.

Looking beyond to Jonah 3, i see the temple on the same bar as the city of Nineveh. Both are constructed, both are earthed places and both have occupants: Yhwh in the temple; and the king, people and beasts in Nineveh. As Jonah was released from the bars of the pit, so was Yhwh delivered from the metaphorical bars of the temple, and i expect the king, people and beasts in Nineveh to also be released from the bars of the city.

Words that move

The reading offered above invites hearing the words and voice of Yhwh (Jon. 1.2) in juxtaposition with the words and voice of Jonah (especially Jon. 2.2-9). Yhwh was brief, rushed and direct; Jonah was deep, rooted and overwhelming. Yhwh moved Jonah to take flight; Jonah moved Yhwh to speak to the fish. The exact words Yhwh spoke to the fish are not given, but they made the fish vomit.

In this narrative, words matter. The words of both Yhwh and Jonah moved them to do something and to say more. The words of Yhwh, like an s-word, sought to cut Nineveh; the words of Jonah sought to deliver Yhwh. The words and voices of Yhwh and Jonah intersect at places that are constructed: Nineveh the great city, the holy temple, the imagined She'ol, deep, pit. In different ways, these places are earth(ed). In this regard, the flow of the narrative into the sea is not about flowing into no-place, the abyss of bottomlessness. Rather, the flow into the sea invites seeing the place of the earthed on earth, and by extension seeing the place of both the earth and earthed in the EBC.

Out of the sea

In the sea, no one expects to remain dry. But many people fear drowning in the sea, especially if the sea is deep. In Jonah's *talanoa*, the sea was deep enough for a big fish. Jonah flowed the narrative into the deep sea and Yhwh pushed him to the ("base of the mountain" at the) heart of the sea(floor). But Jonah did not drown. He kept his cool for three days and three nights, and he was delivered onto dry land.

Spending three days and three nights in the belly of a fish would have affected Jonah's body. He would have landed (in Jon. 2.10) smelling and looking like a creature from the sea if not from another world. Compared to the forbidden tree in the garden, Jonah would not have appeared "good for eating and a delight to the eyes" (Gen. 3.6). In appearance and presence, he would have been fishy. Slimy. Gutty. He would not have drawn admiration, but he would have surely caught people's attention (and disgust).

The Jonah narrative echoes the Priestly creation narrative in separating the sea from the "dry land" (the same word is used in Gen. 1.9-10 and Jon. 2.11, יבשה). This separation is not plain and clear-cut for Pasifika natives, because the sea and the dry land connect in our world. What happen on dry land is influenced by what happens in the sea, and vice versa. The interconnection of the sea and the dry land is particularly clear in climate-affected islands like Tuvalu and Kiribati, seen daily in the rising of the sea level and once a month in the king tide (which floods parts of the islands for two to three days at a time).

Pasifika mythologies link water bodies on land (e.g. Sondo for Solomon Islanders, the pool through which the souls of the dead enter the home of the ancestors) to the sea, as well as link mythological homelands beneath the horizons over the sea (e.g. Pulotu for Samoans, the home of the ancestors) to the dry land of the living. Sondo and Pulotu are places to where the ancestors go after death, and the access to both is through the sea. The sea and the dry land are linked, and both function as registers for our ancestors. Whether one is in the sea or on land, one is in the realm of the ancestors. In this connection, Jonah's landing on dry land does not mean that he has left the sea behind.

Back on dry land, one expects the narrative to slow down.

Chapter 3

FLOW INTO NINEVEH (JON. 2.10–4.11)

Nineveh has been anticipated on the horizon since the beginning of the narrative when YHWH's words first happened upon Jonah (Jon. 1.1-2), but the narrative only reached Nineveh after the big fish spewed Jonah "upon dry land" (Jon. 2.10). After the second happening of the words of YHWH upon Jonah (Jon. 3.1-2), Jonah "got up and went [at once] to Nineveh as YHWH had said" (Jon. 3.3).

Against my expectation for the pace to slow down when Jonah landed back on dry land (noted at the end of Chapter 2), the momentum of the narrative picks up speed. The length of time that Jonah actually spent in Nineveh was shorter than the time he spent in the sea. He started "into" Nineveh in Jon. 3.4 (so NRSV and NJPS) and he was out of the city by Jon. 4.5. It is difficult to determine with certainty when he exited from Nineveh, and this has to do with how one translates the וַ-conjunction at the beginning of Jon. 4.5. Two valid translations come in the NJPS ("Now Jonah had left the city") and the NRSV ("*Then* Jonah went out of the city"; my italics), each carrying a different temporal connotation. The NJPS allows for Jonah to have departed from the city earlier (even before YHWH replied in Jon. 4.4), while the NRSV suggests that Jonah departed only after YHWH's reply in Jon. 4.4. Both translations, nonetheless, allow for the possibility that Jonah entered and exited Nineveh within the same day. It was a short visit. He was in Nineveh for one day (see Jon. 3.4a), compared to his three days and three nights in the fish. Jonah's quick exit was due to the quick response of the people of Nineveh (Jon. 3.5). They did not tarry nor look for excuses but acted immediately (in the next verse).

Back on land, Jonah quickly moved into and away from Nineveh. So, on the one hand, one may argue that Nineveh was not the chief concern of the story. Nineveh was only a platform for showcasing and debating the nature of YHWH: YHWH was so generous and forgiving that YHWH pardoned such a wicked city like Nineveh (the debate extends into the book of Nahum).[1] In this line of thinking, the story is revealing regarding Jonah: he stopped running from YHWH's presence and went to Nineveh, but he did not endorse what YHWH did. He gave in to the demand by YHWH, but he did not approve of YHWH. On the other hand, one could argue that

---

1. The place of Jonah in the twelve (so-called minor) prophets, between Obadiah (especially the voice of patience) and Micah (especially the call for justice and mercy) accentuates this debate.

36 *Jonah*

the main concern of the story is Nineveh. The story opens (Jon. 1.1-2) and closes (Jon. 4.11) with Nineveh, and Jonah's debate with Yʜwʜ (Jon. 4.1-11) circles around Nineveh. Even after Jonah moved away from the city, Nineveh remained as a point of reference. In this line of thinking, the story is all about Nineveh. I follow this second line in this chapter, with emphasis on the various *affects* that Nineveh had on the narrator, on Jonah and on Yʜwʜ. How and what did Nineveh (as a great city, with people and animals) teach Jonah and Yʜwʜ, the narrator and readers? I bring this question to my analysis of the "flow into Nineveh" part of the narrative, in five subsections:

(1) Second happening of Yʜwʜ's words concerning Nineveh (Jon. 2.10–3.4);
(2) Nineveh's response to Jonah and God-Yʜwʜ (Jon. 3.5-9);
(3) God's response to Nineveh (Jon. 3.10);
(2') Jonah's response concerning Nineveh (Jon. 4.1-4);
(1') Yʜwʜ's confession concerning Nineveh (Jon. 4.5-11).

As suggested in Chapter 2, the Jonah narrative echoes (or mimics) the Priestly creation narrative in separating the dry land from the sea. The two narratives also accelerate the pace of the account (e.g. in the Priestly creation narrative the account accelerates from the separation of two elements on the first and second days to several elements on the third day and onward) and climax with attention to the animals. Like the humans, the animals too have food for their survival (see Gen. 1.29-30). Similarly, in the case of Nineveh the humans and the animals come together as one at the end of the Jonah narrative (Jon. 4.10-11). In the "flow into Nineveh" the great city that was characterized by wickedness in Jon. 1.2 and addressed as an empty character in Jon. 3.1 gets populated with people and animals (Jon. 3.5-9), and the narrative climaxes with the affirmation of "the beasts" (see also Chapter 4).

Jon. 2.10–3.4

[2.10] Ywh spoke to the fish, and it spewed Jonah upon dry land.
[3.1] The word of Yʜwʜ happened upon Jonah a second time: [2] "Arise, go to Nineveh the great city, and call to it the call that I will say to you." [3] Jonah arose and went to Nineveh, as Yʜwʜ had said.
[4] Nineveh was a great (גדול) city to God, three days to walk. Jonah began to enter the city, one day's walk, and he called, saying, "Until forty days, and Nineveh will be overthrown."

Yʜwʜ was unrelenting. Yʜwʜ does not fool around. Jonah comes out from the sea and faces the *second happening* (or second coming) of Yʜwʜ's words: "Arise, go to Nineveh the great city and call to it the call that I will say to you" (Jon. 3.2). Yʜwʜ had a "call" (shout, scream) to make and Jonah was the one chosen to deliver it. There is no concern for the well-being of the spewed Jonah, physically or

3. Flow into Nineveh

emotionally. Yhwh would fail the test in pastoral care. The words of Yhwh again ambushed Jonah, and this time Jonah caved (Jon. 3.3). This time, compared to the first happening, Yhwh's call is given a content: "Forty days more, and Nineveh shall be overthrown" (Jon. 3.4, NJPS). The "call" of Yhwh concerns an ambush against Nineveh. Expectation is raised, and a timeline is set.

Forty days, however, is a long time. Modern technology warns people of cyclones and severe weather patterns coming in a few days' time, and tsunami waves are predicted, detected and announced minutes and hours before they reach (is)land. Nowadays, people are warned about catastrophes and they prepare for emergencies in a matter of days and hours. While modern technology was not available in the biblical time, the people in the biblical world had their own ways of reading the paths of the wind and predicting climate changes coming their way (see, for example, 1 Kgs 18.41-6). The people in the biblical world, several of whom were prophets, could see disasters on the horizon and prepare to face those in less than forty days. And some biblical characters even tried to change the courses of the climate and the environment (see, for example, Josh. 10.12-15). With respect to the biblical world, the timeframe of Yhwh's call suggests a generous warning rather than a threat of imminent doom. A lot could happen in forty days, including the diversion and weakening (as storms and cyclones do) of the expected catastrophe as well as change in Yhwh's will (see also Chapter 6). Yhwh could even forget before the deadline.

In the metaphorical world of the Bible the number forty connotes a long span of time. Yhwh flooded earth with rain (in the Yahwist account) for forty days and forty nights (Gen. 7.12), the people of Israel wandered for forty years over the distance between Egypt and Canaan (Num. 14.33-4), Goliath challenged Israel twice a day for forty days (1 Sam. 17.16), and David (2 Sam. 5.4) and Solomon (1 Kgs 11.42) reigned for forty years each. Forty was the biblical figure for a long span of time (forty years is equated to one generation). In this connection, while the announced event is expected to be devastating, it is not imminent. There is no hassle in Yhwh's call. There is enough time for Nineveh to evacuate, if they wish. They could move to another city, or to another country, in order to avoid being overthrown together with the city. In contrast to the hassle against Jonah, to arise and go (at once), time was on Nineveh's side. They could pack and leisurely move, with several days to spare.

How Yhwh planned to overthrow Nineveh is not revealed. I assume that it would be some kind of "natural" event because of what happened in the sea earlier (see also Genesis 6–7), but Yhwh also has extraordinary ways of overthrowing cities (e.g. the burning of Sodom and Gomorrah in Genesis 19 and the dismantling of the walls of Jericho in Josh 6) and nations (e.g. the plaguing of Egypt in Exodus 12). Considering Yhwh's plan of action is relevant if Yhwh was serious and intended to overthrow Nineveh as Jonah announced, and it requires readers to trust that what Jonah announced was what Yhwh had said to him (cf. Carden 2006: 442). In other words, as Yairah Amit instructed, this requires readers to trust the narrative (see Amit 2001: 1–9). I too trust the narrative, but i do not treat it as a record of some historical event. In the world of *talanoa*, the narrative is a story, a telling and an invitation for conversation.

In the narrative and *talanoa* worlds, rhetoric and performance do not always coincide. That Yhwh said and was capable of overthrowing Nineveh does not mean that Yhwh intended to do so. I am here wading into the troubled sea of "intentional fallacy," the assumption that one could determine the intention of an author or character. Literary critics have exposed this fallacy for more than forty years now, and i do not seek to enter that debate. While i admit that i cannot determine Yhwh's intention, i at the same time cannot deny that Yhwh had intentions. From the beginning of this story, Yhwh has been direct and intentional. But i cannot be sure if and when Yhwh was serious, or with what was Yhwh serious. I suggest this distinction because i expect Yhwh to be vigilant with the matters that Yhwh deemed serious. Those would be nonnegotiable. But with matters that were not (so) serious, Yhwh might reconsider and change attitude and plan. Two questions thus arise: Was Yhwh serious about overthrowing Nineveh? And second, was Yhwh serious about the call reaching Nineveh?

The forty days' timeframe suggests that Yhwh was not serious about overthrowing Nineveh. Yhwh is here no different from a parent who wants to discipline a child by saying, "Ok, so, by the time I count to forty I expect you to stop doing that. One, two, three . . ." then something interrupts before that parent reaches forty and the counting stops. If the intention was to threaten Nineveh, or to cause a change in Nineveh, a shorter timeframe would have been more effective: "In three days, Nineveh will be overthrown!" A shorter timeframe emphasizes the gravity of the situation. There is no time for fooling around. "Time to clean up, one, two, three!" A shorter timeframe would have stirred the city, to at least know that Yhwh was serious.

Insisting that Jonah himself delivered the call, given what transpired in Jonah 1–2, gives the impression that Yhwh might not be serious. The narrative thus far presents Jonah as someone who tends to flee and "jump ship," so what made Yhwh think that this time Jonah would go to Nineveh? Yhwh's insistence upon Jonah suggests that Yhwh's angst was with Jonah, rather than against Nineveh. This suggestion presents another reading: that Yhwh was serious about the call reaching Nineveh but not for or against the sake of Nineveh. Rather, Yhwh's drive was to see if Jonah would come under the divine shadow (see also discussion of the final section, Jon. 4.5-11). In other words, this was a test to see if Jonah would come on board with Yhwh. This is not an unbiblical suggestion: Yhwh is known to test elected people like Abraham (Genesis 22) and Israel (Deut. 8.2), and some of the faithful ones even demand that they be tested (see Ps. 26.2 and 139.23). Testing one another is common among people in covenants and relationships.

Yhwh's gripe was with Jonah and in his going to Nineveh, Jonah passes the test: "Jonah *obeyed* the word of the Lord and went to Nineveh" (Jon. 3.3a, NIV; my italics). The NJPS passes Jonah with distinction: "Jonah went *at once* to Nineveh in accordance with the Lord's command" (my italics). At this point, Jonah joins the list of the obedient. This is significant because not everyone passes Yhwh's test or is fully obedient to Yhwh. In the larger biblical account, Yhwh's authority has been tested since the beginning. The garden story (Genesis 2–3) sets readers up to

3. Flow into Nineveh

expect human creatures to *disobey* Yʜwʜ. Even Yʜwʜ's curse of the ground (Gen. 3.17b-18) is broken by Cain when he brought "fruit of the soil" (Gen. 4.3). Yʜwʜ did not have control over the creation then, and it is not certain if Yʜwʜ ever gained sovereignty over the creation and life. Many of the faithful people who passed Yʜwʜ's test end up walking away and/or disobeying at other times: Abraham went off to Egypt in the same chapter in which Yʜwʜ assigned the occupied land of Canaan to him and his descendant (Genesis 12); Israel turned away from Yʜwʜ several times (see, for example, Exodus 32), hence their extended sojourn in the wilderness; and David (see, for example, 2 Samuel 11–12) and Solomon (see, for example, 1 Kgs 11.1-13) are famous examples of favoured leaders who also broke from Yʜwʜ's ways. In the context of the biblical account, it is significant that the runagate Jonah obeys Yʜwʜ.

In yielding to Yʜwʜ's words Jonah flows the narrative into Nineveh, "an enormously large city" (Jon. 3.3b, NJPS). This half verse could be read in two ways: that גדול refers to size (Nineveh was geographically large and spacious) or that גדול refers to might (Nineveh was powerful and imperial). Most English translations assume that גדול is about size because of the final clause, "Walk three days [across]." These translations fail to account for a significant preposition in the half verse: "An enormously large/great city *to/for God* (לאלהים), [that takes one to] walk three days [across]." This לאלהים could be read in complementing ways. First, that the city was significant (גדול, great) in the eyes of God (לאלהים). This suggestion is consistent with the understanding of גדל in previous verses (Jon. 1.2, 4, 10, 16, 2.1). In this understanding, God respects the greatness of the city even though God did not approve of the city's wickedness (in Jon. 1.2). The greatness of the city was not on some moral grounds. Rather, the city was great in itself. Second, לאלהים may also be taken as serving a comparative function: the city was "too great for God." This confession builds upon God's respect for Nineveh: the city is too great, that God alone cannot handle it. This confession makes sense of God's insistence that Jonah delivers the message to Nineveh. Both readings affirm the significance of לאלהים ("to/for God"), and together suggest that God needed Jonah's assistance.

The narrator introduces a shift from יהוה (Yʜwʜ, the Loʀᴅ) to אלהים ('elohim, God) in Jon. 3.3b, but translations that pass over לאלהים suppress this obvious shift in the narrative. I note the shift between names here in Jon. 3.3 and highlight that it was the doing of the narrator, rather than bring it up only in Jon. 3.5 and dedicate it to the people of Nineveh. It is simplistic to assume that the narrator uses אלהים because the people of Nineveh (the subject in Jon. 3.5) were not adherents of יהוה. The words in both Jon. 3.3 and 3.5 belong to the narrator, so i take the shift from יהוה to אלהים to be intentional and not because of the shift of location to Nineveh. There are many ways of describing this shift (see, for example, Limburg 1993: 45–7; Jenson 2008: 41–57, 80–93), and i propose that the shift in name (reference) marks a shift in understanding (perception) as well. The narrator teases his readers: Nineveh is too great for God; God is no match for the great Nineveh. God (as Yʜwʜ) was powerful in the sea, but not so with respect to Nineveh. This is not to suggest that God did not have any power over the land also. Rather, it is to affirm that Nineveh was so great.

Space and time intersect in the narrator's voice. The greatness of the city is described in terms of time: three days' walk (Jon. 3.3). The proclaiming of Yhwh's call is located in time: it began when Jonah reached "the distance of one day's walk" into the city (Jon. 3.4a). And Yhwh's call marks a future time: "Forty days more" (Jon. 3.4b). All of these time references have to do with an occasion: when the word of Yhwh "happened to Jonah a second time" (Jon. 3.1). The intersection of space and time conveys movement—this unit is *about* and it *is in* motion—and therefore about shift and change. The narrative changes background and brings the reader to land. Jonah has a change of mind and goes to Nineveh. Yhwh has a change of name and confesses the greatness of Nineveh. And as the narrative flows deeper into Nineveh, the reader expects change in the outlook of Nineveh also.

Much has been made of the impact of Jonah's four Hebrew words (ארבעים יום ונינוה נהפכת) on Nineveh (Jon. 3.4b), but not enough about Jonah waiting until he was one day into Nineveh (Jon. 3.4a) before he started to proclaim Yhwh's call. Was the first one-third of the city empty? Or more appropriately, what kind of people reside at the edges of a great city such as Nineveh? In light of the Rahab (Josh 2) and Naboth (1 Kings 21) stories, i imagine that the people who dwell at the walls and edges of a city to be prostitutes and workers. They are not empty or lowly people, but people who maintain and labour in and outside of the city. They would be the ancient versions of blue-collar workers, people who live and work away from the centres of power and business. They are "small" people. They are like the fisherfolks who live and work along the coast, and field workers who live on the edge of villages towards the bush. Labourers who dwell at the edges maintain the breadbaskets of the city, but they do not benefit from the fruits of their labour nor are they consulted when it comes to community matters. In walking for one day before beginning to proclaim Yhwh's call, Jonah walked pass such people as if they were not worthy of his proclamation and as if they will not understand his words. This is reasonable, as the people of Nineveh spoke a different language and the people at the edges would not have the same opportunities for education as the power holders. Jonah's behaviour nonetheless fuels discrimination against Nineveh. He expected that some of them will not understand, and that some will not be changed. Those people at the fringes are expendable.

Ecological flow

Yhwh was firm against Jonah, but shifted his position with regard to Nineveh the city which, while it is a human construction, i see and read as an *earthed* subject (see Chapter 2). A small but significant difference between the words that happened upon Jonah suggests this shift:

> Arise, go to Nineveh the great city, and call *against* it (עליה), for their wickedness has come to face me. (Jon. 1.2)

> Arise, go to Nineveh the great city, and call *to* it (אליה) the call that I will say to you. (Jon. 3.2)

Yhwh's call in the "flow into the sea" was against (על) Nineveh, but the call in the "flow into Nineveh" was to (אל) Nineveh and it is no longer in response against Nineveh's alleged wickedness. Between Jon. 1.2 and 3.2, the cloak of wickedness dropped from upon Nineveh. Yhwh shifted with regard to Nineveh, and i suggest that what happened in the sea influenced this shift. Jonah's prayer from the gut of the fish has been realized: Yhwh was delivered, in this case from his bitterness against Nineveh. The initial shift in Yhwh's regard for Nineveh was not the result of his merciful characteristic or capacity to repent (see Jon. 3.10 and Chapter 6), but because the sea and the events at sea taught Yhwh something about Nineveh as an earthed subject.

Yhwh learnt to relate to Nineveh differently from the way that he related to Jonah. With Jonah, Yhwh is like the strong-armed character in Emmanuel Garibay's *My Way* (see Figure 3.1). This artwork is Garibay's critique against

Figure 3.1 Emmanuel Garibay, *My Way* (oil on board, 2009). Used with permission of the artist.

persons of authority who insist that their way is the right way, but they do not see nor account for the consequences of their way(s). Set in the context of climate change, the authority figure in *My Way* points his thumbs at himself but he does not see the drowning person in front of him. His eyes are open (compare to the figure in Garibay's *Akademiko*, see Figure 1.4) but they look to the side. His mouth is also open, suggesting that he calls attention to himself with his words as well, but Garibay stretches his nose, blushes his cheeks and gives him a joker's cap. Such a person of authority should not be taken seriously.

In light of Garibay's critique, Yhwh comes across as a character with two faces. With regard to Jonah, Yhwh insisted on his way. Yhwh was rigid. But with regard to Nineveh, Yhwh has begun to shift his position. Yhwh was movable.

At this intersection, i turn back to the Priestly creation narrative. In the Priestly creation narrative, God did not repeat himself before darkness, light, waters, sky, dry land and their manifold hosts, conceded. God spoke once, and they responded. In the Jonah narrative, on the other hand, a second happening (or second coming) of the words of Yhwh took place before Jonah yielded. Juxtaposing the two narratives invites several readings: that earth and its so-called natural components are more open and willing, compared to Jonah, to collaborate with God; that the recalcitrant Jonah discloses romanticizing leanings in the world view of the Priestly writers (who assume that God was in charge and everything will do his bidding); that Yhwh God does not yield to subjects who do not comply. This third reading explains Yhwh's rigidity towards Jonah, as another character who insisted on his way.

The *talanoa* does not end here.

Jon. 3.5-9

[5] The people of (אנשי) Nineveh believed in God, and they called a fast, put on sackcloth, from the great (גדל)[2] to the small. [6] When the word reached the king of Nineveh, he rose from his throne, removed his robe from upon him, put on a sackcloth, and sat upon the dust. [7] He caused it to be cried, and said, in Nineveh, by decree of the king and his nobles (גדל), "Let no human and beast, flock and cattle, taste anything; let them not eat, let them not drink water. [8] Let them, human and beast, be covered with sackcloth, call with might to God, and let each one turn from his evil way, and from the violence in their palms. [9] Who knows, God may turn and relent, and turn from his fierce anger, that we do not perish."

The narrative divides the "people (lit. men) of Nineveh" into two groups, but they responded as one—both the great (גדול) and the small believed (אמן) God (אלהים), proclaimed a fast and put on sackcloth (Jon. 3.5). Before Jonah reached the other

---

2. I follow the usual practice of translating גדול as "the great" in Jon. 3.5 but "the nobles" in Jon. 3.7.

end of the city (he had two more days to cross), Nineveh (through its people) shifted its mind and orientation. Nineveh shifted on day one of Jonah's proclamation, with thirty-nine days to spare. Nineveh was not as difficult as the narrator had led on.

I assume that the "small" people included those at the outer thirds (edges) of Nineveh by whom Jonah silently passed. They would have heard because words and community decisions, as the cliché goes, spread like wildfire over the grapevine. Even the people who did not hear Jonah's voice would have also shifted their position. It is not as important here that they "believed in God," but that they moved, shifted, changed, in response to Yhwh's call. This point is important because of the prejudices against Nineveh as a city (location) with a trait (as a city, it is expected to be a hub of wickedness). It turns out that Nineveh was not really bad. There was no need for someone from outside of the city to overthrow Nineveh; the people overthrew the city on their own (thank you very much!). And it did not take much effort, on the part of Jonah.

Nineveh's shift started with the people, and then the king joined. That the people led the shift is not unexpected, for public and political changes often start from the so-called grass roots (which Donet affirmed with his roots artworks discussed in Chapter 1, see Figures 1.1 and 1.2). In the more recent time, the Jasmine or Dignity Revolution in Tunisia (in 2010–11) was a civil movement, aggravated by a vegetable seller (Mohamed Bouazizi), that led to the ousting of President Zine El Abidine Ben Ali. And the 2016–17 Candlelight Revolution in South Korea, which led to the impeachment of President Park Geun-hye, was in response to protests by ordinary people including tens of thousands of college and high school students. Similarly, in Nineveh, the normal and ordinary people set the change in motion. One could even argue that democracy was already at work in Nineveh.

The king responded to the people's movement: he "arose from his throne, untied (עבר) his robe, put on sackcloth, and sat on ashes" (Jon. 3.6). The details are suggestive: the king stripped himself of two markers of his authority (throne, robe), and put on two indications of lowliness (sackcloth, ashes) that are associated with mourners (people who have experienced loss). He (as king) had more to give up, and he took on more than the people did (it is not mentioned if the people also sat on ashes, and this is not included in the decree that followed). I assume that the king was sincere, and that he had the interest of the city in his mind and heart. He issued a decree that in-scripted all persons (אדם) and beasts (בהמה) to fast (from food and drink), put on sackcloth, cry mightily to God and turn back from the evil ways and injustices of which they were guilty (Jon. 3.7-8). The king was not fooling around. His intention was clear: "Who knows, God may turn (שוב) and relent (נחם) and turn (שוב) back from his fierce anger, so that we do not perish?" (Jon. 3.9). The king sought to change God's mind and heart as well as God's action. In fact, the king and people of Nineveh showed that the complete change (overhaul) of mind and purpose that they sought from God was possible. They did so themselves. They wanted God to do as they have done and, if needed, they are models for God. They wanted God to mimic what they have done.

The overhaul that Nineveh sought requires unison of "mind" and "heart," which some people in the modern time differentiate: "mind" is understood as referring to matters of cognition and intelligence, whereas "heart" is taken as referring to matters of emotion and feeling. In the Korean language, the unison of intelligence and emotion is realized in the word *ma-eum* (마음) which translates as mind-and-heart (as one). There is no separation between mind and heart in *ma-eum*, a term that reflects the Confucius concept of *xīn* (Kim 2017: 127–8). The significance of *ma-eum* to Koreans is embodied in the short speech that Kim Jong-Un (leader of North Korea) delivered at the historic meeting of the two leaders of North Korea and South Korea on April 27, 2018: Kim used the word *ma-eum-gajin* (the root word for which is *ma-eum*) seven times in his three-and-a-half minute speech. The opening of the border at the Demilitarized Zone (DMZ) between, and the hope for the reunification of, North and South Korea depends on how Korea's *ma-eum* moves.

Drawing from Korea's language and Confucius culture, the *ma-eum* of Nineveh shifted. The people and the king repented and turned back from their evil ways and injustices, and they expected God to also repent and turn from the evil planned against them and their city. In other words, the king and people of Nineveh were seeking a change, a turn, in the *ma-eum* of God.

Given the ease with which the *ma-eum* of Nineveh changed, another possible explanation emerges for Jonah's pass over the edges of the city: Jonah did not proclaim against the workers and labourers at the edges because they were not as wicked as the people at the centre of the city. The king's decree was issued on behalf of himself and the nobles (גדול, the great; Jon. 3.7), and this reference presumes that Nineveh was a classist society. Between the nobles and the workers at the fringes (among the "small" people) are the traders and business people (who, with the nobles, belong to the "great" people), who could easily be corrupted into "evil ways" and become "guilty of injustices." Appealing to Hinduism's caste system, the traders (Vaishyas) come in between the nobles (Kashatriyas, which includes the warriors) and the labourers (Shudras, or service providers). The nobles benefit from the traders, who take advantage of the labourers. In this connection, Jonah's pass over the labourers could have been because they are not the cause of YHWH's anger.

An alternative reading takes the "beasts" in the king's decree as a metaphor for people who are not accepted as civil subjects in the eyes of the king and the nobles. They are non-subjects like slaves, stateless refugees (who are not recognized in the land where they seek asylum) or the Dalits in Hindu societies. The Dalits (the so-called untouchables) have no place in the Hindu caste system, but the Hindu society stands upon their bodies and labour.[3] Dalits do not belong to, and they cannot be reborn into, a caste. They are treated as the cause and embodiment of defilement and ironically, given Hinduism's emphasis on reincarnation, they are

---

3. Drawing upon Garibay's *My Way* (see Figure 3.1), the Dalits is the platform on which the joker stands to rise above the flood.

stuck in the state of defilement. Dalits cannot move up, and there is nothing below them. If people like Dalits, slaves, refugees and workers at the fringes are the "beasts" in the king's decree, then they have a role to play in the survival of the city. The city depends and stands on their shoulders. Their function in the future of the city is recognized, but their non-subjectivity (stereotype, stigma) has not changed. In this reading, the "beasts" are named and decreed to do as noble humans do for the sake of saving the city, in the interest of the king and the noble-greater-upper-class. In this regard, the *ma-eum* of Nineveh has not fully shifted. The modern equivalents of the king's "beasts" are the poor, hungry and sickly children whose images are used by some aid services to draw the sympathy and donation from people of good will. Those are imageries used to move the *ma-eum* of viewers and readers.

This section closes with hope for Nineveh—if the *ma-eum* of God shifts—but the apparent classicist make-up of the city is troublesome. As with all cities, this great city had divisions and internal points of discrimination. It may have been democratic, but it was not a perfect city. Whether it deserved to be overthrown is one question; and whether it deserved to be spared is a different question altogether. Concerning the first question, many commentators consent that it should be overthrown primarily because Yhwh declared (but did not explain why) that it was a wicked city and also because Nineveh was a non-Israelite city. It did not belong to Israel, so it could be overthrown (and no justification was necessary). And concerning the second question, it boils down to whether the change by the city was enough to warrant pardon. Was the change of direction and turn of the city enough to make Yhwh turn as well?

The noble (גדול) class comes through well in this section of the narrative. The narrator named them together with the "small" people in Jon. 3.5 and the king roped them in for the purpose of authorizing his decree in Jon. 3.7-9. They have a lot to save with the sparing of the city, and one could argue that their interests lurk behind the king's "my way" decree.

Ecological flow

With the nobles (גדול), the king too had a lot to save from the sparing of the city. He did not hear Jonah's proclamation first-hand, but he believed the "people of (אנשי) Nineveh" and he did a little more than the rest. He sat on ashes (Jon. 3.6). This posture is seen as a sign of humility and contrition in Pasifika,[4] but i have second thoughts on whether the king sat with a sincere frame of reconciling mind.

---

4. In Samoa, for instance, when someone seeks pardon for a severe wrong, they come and sit on the ground in front of the home of the victim, pull a mat over themselves and cry for pardon. They are usually accompanied by the extended family. This ritual is called *ifoga*, and it could take many days before pardon is given, indicated by the victim lifting the mat from over the offender. The parties could then reconcile.

46   *Jonah*

Who did he want to see him sit on ashes? On second reading, did the king put on an act for the sake of sparing the city for his (and his nobles') welfare?

The king used Nineveh the *earthed subject* for his own interests, similar to the way that humans use and abuse the natural resources of earth. In this reading, the king transferred the Priestly decree for humans to have dominion and rule (Gen. 1.26-8) from the creatures of creation unto the city of Nineveh. The king may have fulfilled the Priestly agenda, but that agenda remains ecologically destructive (see White Jr. 1967). This reading flows with sympathies for Nineveh, and it is critical of how the king and nobles used the city (as an earthed subject) to ensure their privileges. Could the ease of seeing authorities abuse the earthed for their own interests facilitate also seeing how earth (as a whole) is abused for human welfare? Could the city be spared without approving the deeds of the king and nobles?

Jon. 3.10

> And God saw what they did, that they turned from their evil way (דרך); and God relented the evil which he said (דבר) to do to them—he did not do.

What Nineveh did worked! "God relented (נחם) the evil which he said to do to them—he did not do" (Jon. 3.10b). It turned out that, in the case of Nineveh, God was not as brutal as in the previous chapters (especially against Jonah, and consequently against the sea). In this way, the text invites reconsideration of imageries and expectations concerning God.

In biblical narratives, the imagery of a repentant God goes back to the flood story. YHWH God *regretted* (נחם) having made humans (Gen. 6.6-7) seeing that all flesh was corrupted (Gen. 6.11-16), so God decided to destroy "all flesh under the sky in which there is breath of life" (Gen. 6.17). Instead of accepting some of the blame, God condemned the creatures. God sent rain for several days to drown earth and kill all living flesh, human and beast (Genesis 7). After the waters receded and the surface of the earth began to dry up, Noah and his family unloaded the ark and offered a sacrifice to God (Genesis 8). They restarted their life on dry ground by killing some of the animals that they were charged to save. Favouring Noah, God responded by entering into an eternal covenant with all of creation and appointed the rainbow as a reminder to not destroy earth again with rain (Gen. 9.1-17). The rainbow was a reminder to the relenting yet forget-able God.

God's *ma-eum* moved, but God did not confess that the flood was a mistake nor regret (with words) bringing it upon humans, trees, beasts and earth. In the story of the golden calf, on the other hand, Moses reasoned with God (Exod. 32.9-13), and YHWH renounced (נחם) the punishment intended against the covenanted people (Exod. 32.14). In renouncing, YHWH affirmed that it was wrong. The psalmists who lament in hope that God would deliver them (see Psalms 23, 35, 139) track in the footsteps of Moses. They too believed that God can be moved to change both *ma-eum* and practice. It was for the same outcome that the king of

Nineveh aimed, and God did not disappoint. God relented (נחם). God moved. God was movable.

God's change of mind-and-heart (*ma-eum*) was not due to some innate quality (sympathy or grace) within God-self. God's relenting was in response, rather than an initiating move. God saw what the people and beasts of Nineveh did, that "they turned (שוב) from their evil ways, and God relented (נחם) the evil which he said to do to them—he did not do" (Jon. 3.10a). God relented because Nineveh had turned. In this connection, God mimicked Nineveh.

There are narratives (e.g. stories of the patriarchs) and codes (e.g. Ten Commandments) about humans needing to mimic God, resulting in developed teachings and doctrines (e.g. *Imago dei*), but in general readers are reluctant to think that God can also be moved to mimic humans. In fact, one of the theological sins in religious and academic circles is "creating God in our (human, worldly) images" (and images come in both material and verbal forms). This was not a problem for the king and people of Nineveh. They provided an opportunity for God to mimic them, and they succeeded. They took a step further than the psalmists who seek to change God's plan and course of action with their laments, for Nineveh became a model for God. In this regard they are in the same rank as Hagar, an Egyptian woman, the one biblical character who gave God a name (Gen. 16.13). Both Hagar and the Ninevites deserve credit for influencing the covenantal God of Israel.

As the narrative flows deeper into Nineveh, it becomes clear that God is not immune to the influence of others. God is open to respond even to the words and actions of people and beasts that do not regularly worship God.

Ecological flow

Two currents intersect in this verse: what "the people" did (on the ground) and what Yhwh planned (in his mind-and-heart). The people changed their "way" or "path" (דרך), and Yhwh repented (withdrew) what he "said" (דבר) he would do, and both of these—the people's way and Yhwh's plan—are described as "evil" (רעה). The controversy in this verse is that the way of the people changed the mind-and-heart of Yhwh, which flows against the traditional expectation that the way of the people will change in order to align with the mind-and-heart of Yhwh.

I refer to "the people" here but the text, using the third-person plural "their [doing, way]" and "they [turned]," is ambiguous concerning who the subjects are. Are the king and nobles included in this collective subject? One answer to this question is in who among the people of Nineveh changed their way, and the king's decree was for "everyone" (איש) to turn back from their evil ways (דרך) and injustices (Jon. 3.8b). However, the decree was issued in the names of the king and the nobles (Jon. 3.7) as if to exclude them from the collective subject (אדם in Jon. 3.7 but איש in Jon. 3.8) that is charged to save the city. I am thus inclined to see the "normal people" as the subjects whose turn from their evil path caused Yhwh to change his evil mind-and-heart. In this reading, the collective subject in Jon. 3.10 includes lower-classed people and labourers, as well as native and indigenous

48   *Jonah*

people in Nineveh—they are the normal people. They would find evacuating from Nineveh difficult, even within the forty days' deadline. They may not have a lot to move, but they do not have the resources needed to reestablish themselves in another land. They have a lot to gain, compared to the king and nobles who had a lot to save, from the sparing of the city.

The controversy in this reading is the suggestion that the normal people of Nineveh caused the mind-and-heart of YHWH to change. The mind-and-heart of YHWH changed because of what happened on the ground (דרך, way, path), at the grass roots, the doing of the normal people of the ground.

Jon. 4.1-4

> [1] It was evil (רע) to Jonah, a great evil (רעה גדולה), and it grieved (חר) him. [2] He prayed to YHWH saying, "Oh YHWH, Is this not what I said while I was still upon my ground (אדמה)? Therefore, I fled before hand to Tarshish because I knew that you are a gracious-God, slow to anger, with much kindness, and relenting (נחם) against evil (רע). [3] Please, YHWH, take my life, for it is better that I die than live." [4] YHWH replied, "Is your grief (חר) good?"

YHWH chased Jonah into the sea and then pushed him into Nineveh, but turned from Jonah in this section. At first reading, the exchange in this section does not add up. Jonah affirmed the goodness of YHWH in one verse (Jon. 4.2) and in the next verse (Jon. 4.3) he said something which suggests that he did not really believe what he had just said. Jonah prayed praising YHWH for being merciful and forgiving but then he asked YHWH to kill him off in the next verse. There is no connection between his affirming prayer and his chilling request. If he believed that YHWH was gracious, kind, slow to anger and renouncing punishment, then why did he think that YHWH would take his life? Didn't Jonah expect YHWH to be gracious and forgiving towards him as well? Jonah had been "to hell and back," and his chilling request added another layer to his attempt to flee from the presence of YHWH. His flight to the distant port (Tarshish) was scrambled, and this time he directed his flight to the home of the ancestors (see Chapter 7).

YHWH's response is even more strange when heard with a modern twist and reduced to a one-word question—"Really?" YHWH was not sure if Jonah was serious and whether any good will come out of his grief. In other words, "Really, Jonah, is your grief good (for whom)?" In this reading, the exchange between Jonah and YHWH does not click (connect). Something seems missing, or what connects YHWH's response to Jonah's request and affirmation is not obvious. Something in what had happened caused Jonah grief (Jon. 4.1), but the narrator does not name the object of his grief, whether it was towards YHWH, Nineveh or both.

While YHWH and Nineveh are connected in what transpired earlier, what came next suggests that the compassionate and repentant natures of YHWH were not the primary object of Jonah's grief: Jonah expected YHWH to be kind and relenting

(Jon. 4.2b), so he was not surprised by the shift in Yʜwʜ's *ma-eum* towards Nineveh. In this reading, the problem was not that Yʜwʜ repented (which was not strange in the world of the Bible). It appears that the "great evil" (Jon. 4.1a) in Jonah's eyes had something to do with the connection between Nineveh and Yʜwʜ.[5]

I have suggested in the previous section that the king and people of Nineveh made Yʜwʜ mimic what they did, and this is one possible object of Jonah's grief. The drama in Nineveh was not that the king decreed the beasts to do as the humans do, which would have been a spectacle, but that the king also thought that Yʜwʜ would, like the beasts, mimic the people of Nineveh. Did Jonah see the unfolding of this drama and became grieved because of it? If this was the case then Jonah was right in his grief, for Nineveh turned Israel's God into a puppet. This reading makes sense of Jonah's request for Yʜwʜ to take his life. He would rather die than to deal with a God who is a puppet for other (unorthodox) people.[6]

Whereas the people of Nineveh changed their way in response to Yʜwʜ, Jonah held on to his old expectation and understanding of Yʜwʜ. Nonetheless, both the people of Nineveh and Jonah grieved on account of Yʜwʜ. The people of Nineveh grieved because of the evil that Yʜwʜ planned to do to them, and Jonah grieved because "the most compassionate" Yʜwʜ mimicked the people of Nineveh. In light of this difference, the Jonah narrative does not pin Yʜwʜ down to one clear imagery. Yʜwʜ is the most compassionate, and a puppet, as well as a troubler (cause of grief) in different ways to different subjects.

Ecological flow

Jonah's grief was *grounded*: he concluded that what he expected while he was still at his home ground was confirmed in what happened in Nineveh. He understood what Yʜwʜ had done, but he did not approve it.

Furthermore, on another plane, Jonah was *grounded* by his tradition that he could not see Nineveh differently, as in the reading proposed in the previous section: that the turning of the normal people, who were at the fringes of the city, caused Yʜwʜ to repent and spare the city. Jonah remained consistent with the reading proposed in Chapter 2—he bypassed the normal people because he did not think they had any value or influence. In this regard, they proved Jonah wrong by causing Yʜwʜ to change his mind-and-heart towards Nineveh.

The question at the end of this section suggests that for Yʜwʜ Jonah's grief was not well (Jon. 4.4). Out of concern for the earth(ed) subjects, i read Yʜwʜ's question as a critique of traditions and adherents who expect Yʜwʜ to be consistent

---

5. That Jonah fled to a "distant land" (Tarshish) suggests that the foreignness of Nineveh was not the critical issue. He could cope with foreign people.

6. This is made worse by the fact that the people of Nineveh count among those who are called "uncircumcised" in the Bible, such as the Philistines in Judg. 14.3. They are people who are both outside of the covenanted (cf. Gen. 17.14) as well as despised.

50 *Jonah*

(including being consistent with changing his mind) rather than engaged and affected (see Chapter 5). Occasionally, then and now, the earth(ed) subjects require compassionate authorities to relax from their "my way" stance and mimic unorthodox (uncovenanted, non-human and earthed) subjects.

In this section, Yhwh started to *turn* from Jonah. Yhwh chased Jonah into the sea and Nineveh, but here pushed away from Jonah.

Jon. 4.5-11

[5] Jonah had then gone up from the city and sat east of the city. He made a booth there, and he sat in the shade under it, looking for what the city would become. [6] Yhwh-God provided a bush which grew over Jonah, to give shadow over his head and rescue him from discomfort. Jonah was exceedingly (גדל) happy over the bush. [7] But God provided a worm the next day at dawn, which attacked the bush and it withered. [8] And when the sun rose, God provided a burning east wind; the wind blew on Jonah's head, and he became faint. He asked his life (נפש) to die, saying, "Better that I die than that I live." [9] And God said to Jonah, "Is there good in your grief over the bush?" And Jonah said, "Grief is mine, until death."

[10] Then Yhwh said, "You cared for the bush, which you did not work for and you did not cause to grow (גדל), which appeared in the night and perished in the night. [11] And should I not care for Nineveh, the great city, in which dwell more than one hundred and twenty thousand persons (אדם) who do not know between right hand and left hand, and many beasts."

Jonah had gone out of Nineveh, and he took a sitting position east of the city. In Pasifika, anyone who sits down to observe or to speak to another is perceived as a respectful subject (see Havea 2004). Jonah would thus be seen as someone who exhibits one of the signs of being a "real native" in Pasifika, and this is in contrast to his speaking while walking (*lea tu'u* is disrespectful) on the streets of Nineveh. In this section Jonah sat down to observe, to see what becomes of the city and to be respectful in the ensuing events.

The plot of the narrative becomes satirical, with some *giving* and *taking*: first, Yhwh gave a bush, which made Jonah exceedingly happy. Second came dawn and with it Yhwh gave a worm that took away the bush. Third came the sun along with a fierce wind that Yhwh gave to beat Jonah to the point of fainting. At this point, Jonah's request made sense: he was in great pain, and the narrator names Yhwh as the cause of his pain. Yhwh gave the bush to rescue, and then gave the worm and the wind to trouble, Jonah. It thus makes sense that Jonah's request was not to Yhwh, as in the previous section, but to his own life (נפש)—to die! With respect to his request for death, Yhwh turned from Jonah in the previous section and Jonah turned from Yhwh in this section.

Yhwh is very controlling both in the narrative and over the reading of the narrative. I pointed to an example of Yhwh controlling the reading of the narrative earlier, when Yhwh declared (but did not explain) that Nineveh was wicked and readers trust Yhwh's judgement. In this final section, too, Yhwh controlled the reading of Jonah's second wish to die. First, Yhwh responded to Jonah's request as if it was directed at himself. Yhwh "stole" Jonah's request from his own נפש. Second, Yhwh directed Jonah's grief at the bush, but Jonah's grief was with what Yhwh had done—giving and taking the bush, the worm and the wind. Yhwh thus shifted the blame away from himself. And third, Yhwh drew readers' attention away from Nineveh and made Jonah the problem. Jonah sat down and drew the attention of readers to Nineveh, but Yhwh turned readers towards Jonah and made him an emotionally disturbed character (see March 2014: 191). There is no ambivalence here. Yhwh was serious. Yhwh brought Jonah under the divine shadow, and readers go along with Yhwh's drive.

Yhwh gave the final word in the section, and the book: Jonah's alleged concern for the bush (Jon. 4.10) was no comparison to Yhwh's concern for Nineveh (Jon. 4.11). Yhwh gave more value to Nineveh, even though it consisted of 120,000 people who did not know the difference between the right hand from the left hand (a nicer way of saying that they were simple or stupid), as well as beasts. I however cannot be sure if Yhwh's concern for Nineveh was sincere, or merely a platform for getting at Jonah and for bringing Jonah under Yhwh's shadow.

Yhwh's closing words (Jon. 4.10-11, which could be rendered as an assertion or as a question) problematizes Nineveh's "turn": if the people of Nineveh were so stupid not to know right from left, then what value was their turning from their wicked and unjust ways in Jon. 3.5-9? In this regard, in Yhwh's eyes, the people of Nineveh are no better than "beasts" (whether understood literally or metaphorically). At the end of this section, Jonah was silenced but i imagine that he would have seen what became of the city: the city was spared and Yhwh justified why it was spared. *Deliverance was for Nineveh*. If it was up to Yhwh, i would have to read the story accordingly.

Ecological flow

At the end of the narrative, Yhwh shifted the attention to the withered *leaves* of the bush and to the simple people and the many beasts who were the *roots* of the city. The ecological flow of Jon. 2.11–4.11 is clear as the narrative flows into and away from the earthed city of Nineveh and then into the friable ecosystem in the hinterland. The voice and will of Jonah surfed, so to speak, upon the flow of the narrative. His voice was heard, embraced and debated, then silenced, but his body thus far remained unnoticed in this EBC study. A nagging question thus remains at this point: Did the body of Jonah contribute anything towards making the normal or simple people of Nineveh turn from their evil way?

I will return to this question and whether the body of Jonah helped "heal" the city (see Chapters 5 and 7), but for now will simply register here a leaning: it is not enough for an EBC study to stop with the voice, whether of Jonah, of Yhwh, or of earth(ed) subjects. An EBC study would benefit from also listening to the body, including the bodies of plants and beasts (which are recognized and valued at the end of the Jonah narrative) and the body of the ground that receive withered bodies and listen to unheard voices. These unnoticed bodies are like hidden transcripts (Scott 1990: 106); they are presumed and at the same time concealed by the narrative, but they have something to say which often resists and undermines the dominant narrative. I engage with such bodies in the following chapters in which i read the narrative backward, from the end.

Out of Nineveh

The flow of the narrative ended outside of Nineveh, away from where Jonah had entered the city. The narrative opened and closed with the words and voice of Yhwh, but Yhwh changed and moved between the opening and the closing of the narrative. Yhwh moved from seeking to overthrow wicked Nineveh to speaking up on behalf of delivered Nineveh, and from chasing Jonah to turning away from Jonah.

The narrative flows beyond the dry land of Nineveh to a place yonder where Yhwh silenced Jonah. The person that was called and chased in order to go and deliver words was at the end, out of Nineveh, shut up. If it was up to Yhwh, i too would have to shut up.

Part II

FLOWING BACKWARD

Jonah's interpretive history is a richly complex and highly contested one, to which could be added the vast world of popular culture where Jonah surfaces in Melville's *Moby Dick*, Orwell's essays, and even an episode of *Northern Exposure* .... Jonah's story is one that invites constant rereading and appropriations. (Carden 2006: 465)

Chapter 4

BEASTS THAT MATTERED (JON. 4.10-11)

When a narrative reaches the end, readers expect the plot and stories to climax, the tensions to resolve, the ambiguities to make sense and the main characters to live happily ever after.[1] The end of a narrative is thus expected to hold something significant for (understanding) what that narrative is about. This expectation warrants reading a narrative from its end as well.

At this confluence, i make two confessions: first, that reading backward already took place in the *reading forward* parts of this study (e.g. reading the Jonah narrative backward to the Priestly narrative) and second, that *reading backward* (in terms of the plot) involves *reading beyond the limits* of the narrative into other stories and other narratives. There were elements of reading backward in the process of reading forward, and there will be elements of reading forward (e.g. into the Qur'an) in the process of reading backward. Moreover, reading (whether one's orientation is backward and/or forward) is an exercise that involves crossing narrative limits. To read is to step through (read: transgress) the limits of the narrative that one reads.

In this chapter i flow along with Gerald West's reckoning that reading "the book of Jonah from its odd ending" might help make sense of the narrative (West 2014: 729). Reading Jonah from its end has been undertaken by several critics for historical, literary, postmodern and other reasons. It is not my intention to again present a survey of those readings (see West 2014), which i very much appreciate, but i offer two general observations in relation to those works. First, the majority of scholars who account for Jon. 4.10-11 ignore the final clause—"and many beasts." They come close to but do not touch the tail (end) of the narrative. And although West (who prefers the translation "and many cattle") focused on the final clause, in light of the "cattle culture" of the indigenous people of the Cape (South Africa) and their unwillingness to sell or trade their cattle to the Dutch settlers, he did not reach a satisfying conclusion (by resolving the tensions in the closing section and, so to speak, capturing the beasts):

---

1. I distinguish "narrative" from "story" because, at least in Pasifika, each narrative has many stories (e.g. story of Jonah, story of Nineveh, story of Yhwh, story of the bush, and so on) and each story has their own plots and agendas. This distinction applies to both written and oral texts.

56   *Jonah*

But perhaps the final phrase, tenuously linked to the rest of the book by a grammatically indeterminate *vav*, is a reminder of the dangers of trying to make sense of the other. God and Jonah, each in their own way, are trying to make the Ninevites conform to their perspectives; similarly, van Riebeeck and the Company [referring to Dutch settlers and their business] strive, day after day, to make the indigenous peoples of the Cape fit their frame. Perhaps the final phrase in the book of Jonah is a reminder of the otherness of the other. (West 2014: 748)

For West the many cattle at the end of the Jonah narrative function metaphorically, pointing to and through the other (cattle as other) to the state of otherness (otherness of cattle). This metaphorical leap brings to mind the relation between foreign or strange bodies (e.g. cattle) and the trouble that some people have with their foreignness (i.e. otherness). This raises a simple question for me: Why can't the final clause simply be about the beasts (cattle) themselves? I raise this question because, and this is my second observation, the few readers who deal with the final clause of the book tend to take it metaphorically (including my reading in Chapter 3, where i suggested that the "beasts" was a metaphor for the "simple" people of Nineveh). For the majority of readers who lean towards this orientation, the beast metaphor is a platform for highlighting the mercy of God which extends beyond the human realm into the realm of animals (see, for example, Shemesh 2010). These readers are selective with who was (not) a metaphor. God (*qua* being) was gracious even to the beasts (*qua* metaphor) and through the beasts to the animals, and then through the animals to God.

In this chapter, i look at the "beasts" (*b'hemah* in Jon. 4.11) as referring to both beasts themselves and as a metaphor for all animals. I too look through the beasts, but not towards God. Rather, i look through the beasts towards other animals in general. The grouping of beasts with other animals goes back to the Priestly creation account (see Gen. 1.24-5), which Habel calls the *Erets* myth (Habel 2011: 20),[2] to which i again return—to again read backward—in the following section.

Earth's b'hemah

Most scholars agree that, according to the Priestly creation account, the world was not empty when Elohim began to create the heavens and the earth (Gen. 1.1). The view that the creation was *ex nihilo* (out of nothing, see Anderson and Bockmuehl 2018), whether by a super-being or as the result of a big bang, cannot be sustained on the basis of the Priestly account. But scholars are not of the same mind if Elohim created alone, with his own life-giving and magical words, or

---

2. Habel prefers to use "myth" (as genre), but i opt for "account" and "narrative" in order to sidestep the default assumption that myths are not factual and untruthful. While many accounts and narratives are not factual and untruthful, their literary status gives those some weight in literary-preferring cultures.

received assistance and directions from other creators. The reading that i prefer is based on the observation that in the Priestly account the Waters and the Earth are the co-creators whom Elohim called upon to collaborate in creating humans in Gen. 1.26 (see also Havea 2019a).[3] The creation did not unfold in response to a solo by Elohim. Elohim did not create alone (so Habel), but called on the Waters and the Earth to help "let [structures, features and creatures] *be(come)*" or "come forth" and consequently the heavens took shape and the earth and the waters were cleared and organized, and then planted, populated and animated. The creation was a team effort, a collaboration.

My concern here is with the beasts, and the significance of the role they played in the Priestly creation narrative. The "beasts" (*b'hemah* in Gen. 1.24) were among the second set of beings that Earth brought forth. While i agree with Habel that Earth is a significant character and a co-creator with Elohim (Habel 2011: 26, 33), i divert from Habel because i do not see Earth as a newborn or a secondary creator who jumps up in the service of Elohim (Habel 2011: 33–4). In the Priestly account, Elohim did not (pro)create Earth. On the other hand, Earth is primordial. Earth was in the deep, under the covers of darkness and of the waters (Gen. 1.2). I therefore imagine a rescue event in the Priestly account, echoed in many stories told in relation to migration, resettlement and asylum seeking. Elohim asked the Waters to move aside so that Earth could *surface* (Gen. 1.9-10). When the Waters moved from upon the *face* of Earth, it became apparent that Earth was not void or formless. Earth was living. It had life within it, and Elohim called upon this faculty on day three: "Let Earth sprout vegetation" (Gen. 1.11), and Earth did not disappoint. Earth *brought forth* vegetations of different kinds (Gen. 1.12) and "Elohim saw that this was good" (Gen. 1.13). I take this affirmation to mean that Elohim approved both the vegetations that began to clothe Earth and the ability of Earth to generate (bring forth) life.

It was Elohim's idea that Earth be clothed with vegetations, but it was Earth's own doing to *green* itself. In this connection, Earth was not "young and free" (a phrase from the national anthem of Australia) but ancient and life-giving. I resist saying here that Earth was like a mother (as natives are expected to say) because the mothering role assumes that one starts with a (pro)creating partner. In the Priestly account, Earth was self-generating. On day three, Earth on its own brought forth the vegetations.

The beasts came on day six. Again, Elohim "said" a request directed at Earth: "Let Earth bring forth every kind of living life" (Gen. 1.24). On this occasion, *b'hemah* is the first and the only one to be specified in the report of Earth's offspring: "And Elohim made living beings on Earth of every kind, beasts (*b'hemah*) of every kind, and all kinds of beings that creep on the ground (*'adamah*). And Elohim saw that this was good" (Gen. 1.25). Elohim affirmed the life-giving capacity of Earth at

---

3. I do not follow Habel in separating the *Tselem* myth (Gen. 1.26-8) from the *Erets* myth. Gen. 1.26-8 has a critical place in my reading of the Waters and Earth as co-creators with Elohim.

the beginning of day six, and i see Earth among the co-creators of 'adam in Gen. 1.26. How 'adam is an image of Elohim is debatable, but there can be no denying that 'adam is an image of Earth (the Yahwist narrative supports this suggestion, see Gen. 2.4b-7). In this reading humans, both male and female, are among "every kind of living life" that Elohim asked Earth to bring forth at the beginning of day six, the first of which are the beasts. The beasts are older siblings of humans in the Priestly story; hence, put differently, humans and beasts are in the same race.

This reading could be supported with science and history, but my drive is not whether the biblical account is factual, truthful or scientific. Rather, my drive here is to entertain possible explanations for why beasts have a special place in the closing words of the Jonah narrative. And in this brief look back to the Priestly narrative, one explanation emerges: beasts were among the firstborns of Earth, before the humans. This makes sense of why YHWH-Elohim was concerned about beasts.

Since beasts and animals have legs, they were "brought forth" differently as compared to the vegetation. This is suggested by the different Hebrew words used: דשא (sprout) for the vegetation in Gen. 1.11 but יצא (go or come out) for the beasts and animals in Gen. 1.24. The vegetation were caused to sprout (and to become great, גדל, similar to the bush as described in Jon. 4.10), while the beasts and animals were led out into the presence of Elohim.[4] Earth did both the sprouting and the leading out, and the narrative allows for the possibility that the beasts existed prior to Elohim's request. Earth's b'hemah existed prior to the occurrence of Elohim's words, and Earth knew where to find them and led them out. In this regard, YHWH-Elohim's concern for the beasts in Jon. 4.10-11 could also be out of respect for Earth.

YHWH Behemoth

Grammatically, Behemoth is the plural of b'hemah (both are feminine in form) so it could be considered as a conglomeration of b'hemah. In this connection, Behemoth is like an empire if understood in the way that Joerg Rieger defines empire as "conglomerates of power that are aimed at controlling all aspects of our lives, from macropolitics to our innermost desires" (Rieger 2007: vii). Putting Behemoth and empire in the same frame would draw fearful and disgusting reactions, as well as some subversive and resisting responses. While those responses are appropriate with respect to empire (see, for example, Havea 2018a, 2019b), they do not do justice to Behemoth.

A different picture of the Behemoth could be seen in the shadows of Job (see especially Job 40.15-24). After Job's attempts (in the debates with his three friends

---

4. Compare with the story of Cain (who brought forth fruit of the ground) and Abel (who brought forth firstlings of his flock) in Gen. 4.3-4, but the word used there is בוא (to come in, to enter).

in Job 3–31) to draw Yhwh out of silence, and after young Elihu's intervention to shut Job down and to put him in his place (Job 32–7), Yhwh replied from the tempest beginning with Job 38. Yhwh was not happy, and Job received a verbal lashing for two chapters. Job then bowed out (Job 40.1-5), but Yhwh continued, bringing Behemoth (Job 40.15-24) and Leviathan (Job 40.25-32) in to make the point that Job was nothing (similar to the simple people of Nineveh) compared to these powerful creations of God. Behemoth "is the first of God's works" (Job 40.19, NJPS) and is as strong as Leviathan: "Lay a hand on him, and you will never think of battle again" (Job 40.32, NJPS). Leviathan appeared earlier in Job 3.8 (and four other places in the Bible: Ps. 74.14, 104.26, and twice in Isa. 21.1) but Behemoth has only one appearance in the Hebrew Bible, in Job 40.15-24. The message is clear: Job does not stand a chance against Behemoth or Leviathan, and Yhwh is more fierce than both of them together (Job 41.2). The descriptions of Behemoth and Leviathan together strike fear in readers, and that seems to be the impact for which Yhwh was drilling. But if one reads the descriptions separately, the two beasts are not as frightening. Reading backward, i begin with Leviathan.

The description of Leviathan in Job 40.25-32 amounts to a warning—do not attempt to lay a hand on him. One cannot draw Leviathan out, press his tongue down or put a ring through his nose (in order to lead him around); Leviathan will not plead or speak soft words, agree to be a slave, let anyone play with him as a pet or allow traders and merchants to sell him (in whole or in parts). This is fair enough, for no one should do harmful things to any living creature or expect them to quietly lie down at the slaughter house or market. In the case of Leviathan, size matters. Leviathan is so huge that one cannot "fill his skin with darts or his head with fish-spears" (Job 40.31), and so it is futile to think that one can control him. One cannot tame or overcome Leviathan, so it is best to leave him alone—Job and readers are thus warned.

Leviathan is big and strong, but nothing in his description in Job 40.25-32 suggests that he is reckless or ruthless. He might be "elusive" and "twisting" (Isa. 27.1, NJPS), but Yhwh created him to sport in the sea (Ps. 104.26) and then crushed and fed him to the "denizens of the desert" (Ps. 74.14, NJPS). In the other biblical texts that name Leviathan, he is presented as vulnerable and a victim. Fear of him is thus unfounded in biblical texts. He has a bad rap among readers who by default expect him to be a monster instead of a gentle giant and predecessor to, for example, DreamWorks' Shrek, the green ogre, or Hagrid in J. K. Rowling's *Harry Potter* novels. At the mention of his name, and without even reading his description, readers expect Leviathan to be destructive (similar to the way Disney characterizes Maui the Pasifika demigod in *Moana*). Interestingly, readers who see Leviathan as a monster do not also see Yhwh, who according to Job 41 is much stronger than Leviathan, as a more terrible monster. In other words, such readers do not follow through with the consequences of their reading.

Moving back to Job 40.15-24, we find Behemoth to be a complex character. Yhwh made Behemoth, as well as Job. Behemoth's size is not an issue, as in the case of Leviathan; on the other hand, the glory of Behemoth is in his might and strength. Behemoth eats grass like other flesh, but he is much stronger, evident

60   *Jonah*

in the muscles of his belly, tail and thighs, as well as in his bones and limbs. Nonetheless, Behemoth has several points of vulnerability (Job 40.19-22): his maker can draw a sword against him, the mountains yield produce for him in the playing field of other beasts who could fight him over the same feed, and he rests in the swamp under the protection of the lotuses (in terms of size, he would not have been terribly big). Behemoth is strong, and vulnerable. His physical strength is matched with his extraordinary ability to control water:

> He can restrain the river from its rushing;
> He is confident the stream will gush at his command. (Job 40.23, NJPS)

Behemoth is vulnerable, but he is not weak. He can restrain the river (but the text does not explain how) and he can command (with words) the stream to gush. The content of river and stream is water, and deep and flowing water is difficult to control. In fact, it is more difficult to control deep and flowing water (implied in Ps. 74.12-17) than to control monsters. Water may not have teeth and claws, or breathes fire, but its power is undeniable. Water can kill fire and drown monsters, and water has a way of slipping through one's grasp. Like water, Behemoth is difficult to control.

There is movement in the description of Behemoth: the description begins with his brute physical strength and moves to his physical vulnerabilities, then shifts to his extraordinary power over water and then ends with his two vulnerable organs:

> Can he be taken by his eyes?
> Can his nose be pierced by hooks? (Job 40.24, NJPS)

These questions point to two locations of power, both of which are small in size—eyes and nose. There are two ways to understand these questions. First, if one understands them as rhetorical questions, then the answer is obvious: No! This answer could be emphatic in light of what was said in the previous verse— it is clearly not possible to control the one who could control water? Second, a different understanding emerges from leaving the questions open. Yhwh raises the questions and invites Job—and by extension, readers—to respond. Job does not give a response, and many readers do not venture a response because they take these as rhetorical questions. I, on the other hand, am moved by the tension between the strength of Behemoth (Job 40.15-18) and his vulnerability (Job 40.19-22). So i hear Yhwh exposing Behemoth's vulnerability in the questions: despite his strength, Behemoth could be chopped up by his maker (Job 40.19b) as well as taken by his eyes and nose (Job 40.24; cf. 40.26). Like Leviathan in Ps. 74.14, Behemoth is at risk. This understanding of Behemoth flows into the description of Leviathan as presented earlier.

Behemoth is not as big as Leviathan but equal in strength and "untouchability" (by humans). Yhwh's Behemoth, even though a conglomeration of powers (*b'hemah*), is vulnerable. In this brief review of Yhwh's response to Job, Yhwh's concern for beasts in Jon. 4.11 makes sense. Yhwh was concerned for beasts

4. Beasts That Mattered 61

(*b'hemah*) as creatures that YHWH made, prior to and at the same time in the manners of humans and other living beings; and YHWH was concerned for beasts (*b'hemah*) because they are strong but vulnerable.

#b'hemah

A concordance survey shows many occurrences of *b'hemah* and its cognates in the Hebrew Bible (188 times, according to *Strong*), thus warranting that attention be given to it. This EBC study, however, is not a word-study in the traditional way but a reflection on the nuances and impacts that the name tag *b'hemah* presupposes, carries and invites. With respect to this study, the expected apologies and qualifications apply: this study does not pretend to be exhaustive or final.

In this section i draw attention to texts that add, or could be read as adding, further evidence of the vulnerability of beasts. My focus on vulnerability leads from the discussions in the previous section, and also in the interest of naming alternative responses to the name tag "beast." In addition to sentiments of fear and disgust in response to the mention of beast, this study considers the possibility that YHWH in Jon. 4.11 was feeling sorry for (the key ingredient for changing one's mind, which was the target of Nineveh's king in Jon. 3.9) and seeking to be in solidarity with (the key ingredient for communitarianism, the philosophy that expects an individual to be responsible for the collective, which is evident in the efforts of the sailors in Jon. 1.13) vulnerable beasts. The aim of this study is not to replace the reading of YHWH as gracious and merciful in Jon. 4.11 but to complement it. Reading YHWH as gracious in sparing Nineveh, to borrow a gathering image, places all of the eggs in one basket (i.e. in YHWH's "mercy basket"); reading for the vulnerability of beasts adds another basket, namely that there are qualities in the beasts themselves that warrant their delivery. Put differently, there is beauty in the beasts as well.

Other biblical b'hemah

The point of departure for my reflection on *b'hemah* in this section is provided by Isa. 27.1, a text that was already mentioned earlier. Although this text does not name *b'hemah*, i hear hints to *b'hemah* (based on the discussions in the previous sections) in the naming of Leviathan:[5]

---

5. I leap from Leviathan to *b'hemah* on the basis of three textual lures: first, at the end of Isa. 27.1 "Leviathan" is presented as a figure for another creature, Tanin, a move that i take as an opportunity to take Leviathan as a figure for *b'hemah* as well; second, i take the overlap between the descriptions of Leviathan and Behemoth in Job 40 (discussed earlier) as opening for linking Leviathan with *b'hemah*; and third, the double references to serpent (which i discuss later) invite putting Leviathan and *b'hemah* in the same frame.

In that day YHWH will visit
with his great, cruel and mighty sword
against Leviathan, the elusive serpent
and against Leviathan, the twisting serpent
and he will slay Tanin who is in the sea.

In the face of the great, cruel and mighty sword of YHWH, Leviathan was vulnerable. He was marked, like any other living being that has been set aside for the altar or for the slaughter. Leviathan was as good as dead. And so was Tanin, the sea dragon. The fate of one applies to the other; Leviathan and Tanin share the same lot. The juxtaposition of these two "beasts" invites one to expect the same fate for other "beasts" of comparable stature like Behemoth, the conglomeration of *b'hemah*.

The double identification—in case one does not see it the first time, it is repeated—of Leviathan with the serpent brings to mind a creature with the same name (*nahash*) whom the Yahwist narrator presents as "the shrewdest of the living beings of the field (חית השדה) whom YHWH made" (Gen. 3.1, NJPS renders חית השדה as "wild beasts"). The serpent at the garden was indeed wise. He communicated and convinced the humans, through the woman—who must have appeared to be the reasonable one of the two. But YHWH cursed the serpent for revealing to the woman that the forbidden fruit would make her know good and bad like divine beings (Gen. 3.5b). In cursing the serpent, YHWH situated him among and above other animals: "And YHWH Elohim said to the serpent: Because you did this, more cursed are you than all beasts [*b'hemah*] and all living beings of the field" (Gen. 3.14a). The serpent was thus identified in the group of beasts. In this connection, the double identification of Leviathan as a serpent places the vulnerability of both upon *b'hemah*.

YHWH cursed the serpent for doing something that one expects from a shrewd creature—namely, to enlighten fellow creatures—and YHWH did not give any justification for the curse. YHWH did not even ask the serpent for an explanation or to defend his action, which the serpent could have done because he had language, insight and reason. YHWH condemned the serpent without a trial, robbing him of natural justice and treating him as a "simple" creature. I see the curse of the serpent as foreshadow for creatures who are ignored, at the whim of their creator (also in the case of Job 40.19 and Ps. 74.14, discussed earlier). The serpent (who is Leviathan in Isa. 27.1) might have been elusive and twisting, but it cannot escape YHWH's great, cruel and mighty sword. In this connection, the serpent was a prefigure for beasts (like Leviathan and Behemoth) who are vulnerable.

The Genesis flood narrative also highlights the vulnerability of *b'hemah*. YHWH regretted creating human beings (*'adam*), seeing that every plan they devise "was nothing but evil all the time," and he decided to blot out humans as well as beasts (*b'hemah*), creeping things and birds (Gen. 6.5-8). These animals were doomed not because of their own doing, but because they were victims of the evil devices of human beings. I take these animal victims as biblical prefigures for vulnerable creatures—including animals, birds, fish, plants, humans—who are victims of disasters caused by climate change in the current time. The vulnerable victims

4. Beasts That Mattered

who live outside of the major carbon producing societies, who contribute very little to the global carbon count but are forecast to lose the most (if not everything) as a consequence of climate change, receive more than their fair share. Many of the people and animals who live in the low-lying islands of Pasifika, together with the vulnerable islands themselves, are among their numbers. For these vulnerable victims, climate justice is the real struggle. They too are among the cursed beasts.

Several of the references to *b'hemah* in the Pentateuch relate to sacrifices, going back to the flood narratives where they are divided into categories of clean and unclean animals. YHWH instructs Noah to save both clean and unclean beasts (Gen. 7.2), but to sacrifice only clean beasts (Gen. 8.20). Mary Douglas has offered explanations for why animals are clean or unclean in the Levitical codes (cf. Douglas 1966: 42–58), and i will not repeat nor assess her arguments here. What could impact my study are two occasions when the body of a beast makes the human body unclean: first, touching the carcass of a beast (which has died a natural death) that one could eat (so it is a clean beast) makes the toucher unclean until the evening (Lev. 11.39) and second, approaching (Lev. 18.23) or having sex with a beast (Exod. 22.19; Lev. 20.15-16) is an abomination and the guilty person, male or female, shall be put to death together with the beast. In the first case, the beast is already dead (the carcass of a clean beast is clean if it is slaughtered, but defiling if it dies a natural death); in the second case, the beast will be put to death (the text does not rule out the possibility that the slaughtered beast may then be eaten). In the sex scenario, the Priestly legislator does not distinguish between clean and unclean beasts but gives the impression that they are both defiling. Humans may eat but should not have sex with clean beasts; but clean beasts that have been defiled by sexual contact with humans will be slaughtered and may be eaten by humans.[6] Looking at the second case through the experience of beasts, a double phase of victimization is obvious because the beast (male or female) is presented as a passive party in the sexual encounter thus making its slaughter unjust—the beast is a victim of sex, and a victim of slaughter. In these regulations, the beasts are vulnerable.

I extend the above observation into the sphere of rhetoric. Beasts are made vulnerable in biblical narratives in which narrators and characters use "beast" as tag or label. A "living being" that is seen to cause defilement (in biblical codes) or to belong to rival and hostile parties (in biblical narratives) is called a "beast" (*b'hemah*), and this tag serves derogatory functions and conjures insulting affects. I suggest this position on the basis of the two key Hebrew words that could be translated into "cattle"—*miqneh* (מקנה, sixty-three times in KJV) and *b'hemah* (בהמה, fifty-two times in KJV). The two words carry different connotations in their respective narratives. *Miqneh* is used in reference to property, inheritance and status, so that the number of *miqneh* that one owns indicates his wealth (ownership and wealth are associated with males). In the case of Abram, his wealth is identified

---

6. The beast is unclean because of the sexual encounter but would be considered clean in the way it died (slaughtered).

according to his many *miqneh* (see Gen. 13.2) and the conflict between his and Lot's herdsmen had to do with their wealth (Gen. 13.7). The conflict is between two wealthy households, narrated in terms of *miqneh*. While there is conflict, the parties are kin and genial. On the other hand, *b'hemah* is used to refer to rivals (as in the reference that Hamor makes to Jacob's cattle in Gen. 34.23) and enemies (as in the description of Esau's wealth in Gen. 36.3, and in the reference to the cattle in Egypt that were slaughtered in Exod. 8.17-18). In this comparison, in light of the law codes discussed above, the *b'hemah* tag tarnishes if not defiles the wealth of rivals and outsiders.

The choice of *b'hemah* in biblical rhetoric thus comes across as a biblical form of name calling, a maligning practice to which biblical translators contribute. Translators render *b'hemah* as "cattle" when they see an amiable (and edible) picture but translate it as "beast" when they feel unpleasantness in the text. Following this rhetoric and logic, the *b'hemah* tag in Jon. 4.11 is derogatory against Nineveh—it is a city of beasts (*b'hemah*). The text is specific. There might be *miqneh* in Nineveh as well, but they do not matter. The critical question concerning this suggested reading is whether Yhwh's response to Jonah followed this rhetoric. Was Yhwh being consistent, or could Yhwh have used the tag *b'hemah* because, as discussed above, they were known to be vulnerable? This alternative could serve as justification for sparing Nineveh. The vulnerable beasts in Nineveh made Yhwh change his mind about destroying the city.

I use "beast" for the *b'hemah* in Jon. 4.11 in order to foreground the sentiments that the name tag raises, and in the process i upset the usual expectations by showing that *b'hemah* is a vulnerable subject in biblical texts. I consequently raise the possibility that the vulnerability of the *b'hemah* might be the reason why Yhwh showed concern for Nineveh. Yhwh was concerned for the beasts not only because he was gracious and merciful but also because Yhwh was sorry for and in solidarity with the vulnerable beasts. The vulnerability of the beasts is heightened by the sorry state of their human companions: "More than one hundred and twenty thousand persons (*'adam*) who do not yet know their right hand from their left" (Jon. 4.11). Together, the inhabitants of Nineveh are *too vulnerable to be destroyed*. It makes sense in this reading that the city is spared on account of the beasts. The beasts made Yhwh change his mind.

King's b'hemah

There are many beasts in the Jonah narrative. Earlier in the narrative the king of Nineveh ordered that the *b'hemah* (named twice in Jon. 3.7 and 3.8) of Nineveh also join in the fast, put on sackcloth and cry to God (see Chapter 3). The king did not leave the future of the city to the devices of his human subjects alone, but he called for the assistance of the beasts. The king's beasts were not roaming the fields, away from Nineveh's centres of living and the so-called business district. Rather, the beasts were in the city among the people, in the shadows of this earthed empire. The people of Nineveh, great and small, would have been familiar with the king's beasts, and so they would not have an excuse to fear them.

Nineveh's beasts are divided into two groups in Jon. 3.17: among the flock (בקר) and the herd (צאן). They may not have been fully trained and domesticated, but they would have been considered among the clean animals. They could be slaughtered or sacrificed, but those are not the king's agenda. In the eyes of the king, the beasts are not vulnerable (to be protected). Rather, they are agents of change. They have a role to play in changing Yhwh's mind-and-heart and thereby contribute to securing pardon and survival for Nineveh. They may not have access to human language, but their voices and bodies could help Nineveh.

The king's confident and trusting view is different from the usual responses to beasts—fear, disgust or feeling sorry for beasts. There are many responses to the tag name "beast," and there is no reason why one should trump the others. Furthermore, there is no reason why one should reject the possibility of being saved by beasts or the opportunity to be in solidarity with beasts. The king of Nineveh affirmed both with respect to the *b'hemah* of Nineveh.

The ends

In the course of this first chapter of reading the Jonah narrative from its end, it became clear that there are multiple ends from which one reads and as many ends for which one reads (cf. Avalos 2007: 20–6). One reads from and for, for example, textual, oral, ideological, political and other ends. With respect to the scriptural state of the Jonah narrative, i bring this chapter to close by drawing attention to two canonical ends.

Bible's end

From the end of the Jonah narrative, the earthed city together with the simple people and the earthy beasts of Nineveh are presented in the same frame—they all are objects of Yhwh's compassion (חוס, pity, care). Yhwh justified his compassion to these subjects on the basis of the compassion that Jonah extended towards the bush.

No matter how one reads the end of the Jonah narrative (Jon. 4.10-11)—as a rhetorical question or as a climactic exultation—Yhwh was seeking to bring Jonah into his frame of mind-and-heart, under his control and shadow. I know that Jonah is Yhwh's target because i had read the narrative forward, but Jonah is addressed and not named in the end. If one was to read only Jon. 4.10-11, only the end, Yhwh's words are addressed to all readers—inviting and challenging all readers to also show compassion towards the city, the people and the beasts, and not just to the bush. Yhwh's words may be summed up as a question, "Where's your compassion?" This question is inspired by the artwork *Where's the Key?* (see Figure 4.1).

Where's the Key? was created by a group of Pasifika Islanders that called themselves the Youngsolwarans (meaning "young saltwater people") during a seminar at Madang, Papua New Guinea (August 2014). This work depicts the

Figure 4.1 Youngsolwarans, *Where's the Key?* (oil on canvas, 2014). Used with permission of artists.

island of Papua, the largest island in Pasifika, whose shape is similar to the shape of the bird of paradise (head at the west and tail at the east of the island). Papua is divided between two nations, Papua New Guinea (to the east) and West Papua (occupied by Indonesia). The young saltwater group of artists coloured the island with the flags of the two nations and placed a chain with a lock held by a strong arm (representing Indonesia) around the neck of the bird. The title of the work—*Where's the Key?*—challenges viewers to look for the key that will unlock the chain and thus let the bird (Papua) fly again. The work invites viewers to also remove their blindfold (represented by the cloth placed over the "face" of PNG) from the suffering of the West Papuans.

Adapting the Youngsolwarans' question to viewers, i imagine Yhwh at the end of the Jonah narrative asking readers, "Where's your compassion?" I focused on the beasts in this chapter because i will return with alternative readings of the bush, the city and the people in Chapters 5 and 6, but i assert at this intersection that all of these earth(ed) subjects are deserving of compassion.

Qur'an's end

>And We sent him to [his people of] a hundred thousand or more.
>And they believed, so We gave them enjoyment [of life] for a time.
>
>Qur'an (37.147-8, Sūrah Aṣ-Ṣaffāt; SAHIH International)

The Sūrah Aṣ-Ṣaffāt (in six verses) does not contain many of the details of the Jonah narrative that one reads in the Hebrew Bible. The biblical details may have been well known during the time of Mohammed (*'alayhi salām*) and thus not deemed necessary to be repeated, or those details may not have been significant enough to be mentioned. Nonetheless, there are significant insights in the Qur'anic version that create possibilities for rereading the biblical narrative.

Reading the Sūrah Aṣ-Ṣaffāt backward, the reference that Allah (the royal "We" in the text) sent Jonah (Yūnus, *'alayhi salām*) to his own people (a popular reading among Muslims and it is inserted in the cited translation) is inviting. Nineveh was not an enemy territory to Jonah, but his home ground. This is a different picture from the hostile setting presented in the biblical account: in the biblical account Jonah went away from his home ground, but in Sūrah 37.147 and 10.98 he was coming to his people. This is therefore a homecoming, rather than a mission and conversion, story.

Allah showed compassion towards Nineveh because Jonah's people believed, and as a consequence they were given enjoyment (compared to the rhetoric of deliverance in the biblical narrative). Their enjoyment was temporary, only for a limited time. The Qur'an does not expect Nineveh's enjoyment to be eternal, but it at least withdrew the focus from the compassionate Allah (read: YHWH, the subject of interest in the previous section), back to Nineveh (the primary subject in Jon. 4.10-11).

Sūrah Aṣ-Ṣaffāt does not say if Allah sent a message of words through Jonah. It simply states that Allah *sent Jonah* to his people. I understand this to mean that the people did not believe because they received words from Allah but because they received the body of Jonah which was one of their own, a part of their communal whole. The end of the Qur'an text thus answers my question at the end of Chapter 3—whether the body of Jonah contributed to the sparing of Nineveh: Jonah's body did have a contribution at the end of the Qur'an text, as well as at the end of the Hebrew Bible version, as it was because of the body of Jonah that the bush sparked YHWH's closing and silencing response in Jon. 4.10-11. The body of Jonah also points the process of *reading backward* to Chapter 5, to the bush.

Chapter 5

A BUSH THAT MOVED (JON. 4.1-9)

> But We threw him onto the open shore while he was ill.
> And We caused to grow over him a gourd vine.
>
> Qur'an (37.145-6, Sūrah Aṣ-Ṣaffāt; SAHIH International)

The Qur'an opens the shore up, so Jonah did not have to force himself (as colonialists and refugees do) onto land. Since he was coming to his own people (see Chapter 4) i expect the land to be open to him even if some of his own people found him a little strange or disturbing this time (depending, as far as the narrative is concerned, on how long it has been since they last saw him, and on his physical and mental conditions when he landed). Land and people do not always see things and (other) people in the same way, and it is interesting for me as a migrant worker that the Qur'an refers to "open shore" rather than "open land." While shore is interconnected with land, the shore is the place of arrival and departure whereas the land is the location for homemaking, for (re)settlement, for (dis)possession and for profit-making. The shore is the edge, the fringe, the margin, of the land, and the Qur'an opens it up for Jonah. In opening up the shore, the Qur'an also opens up the land for Jonah.

Declaring that Nineveh had an open shore is contrary to the declaration of *terra nullius* (empty land) that colonialists used, then and now, to justify their invasion and occupation of many (is)lands in Pasifika and beyond. The colonialists declared (is)lands to be uninhabited because they did not see the kind of (human) development or (Western) civilization with which they were familiar in their homelands, and the declaration of *terra nullius* in the ears of international law (during the colonial era) was sufficient to justify the colonialists' claim of the "new world" as territory for their crown. Declaring foreign lands as empty allowed the colonialists to also claim that they have "discovered," and therefore have the right to exercise sovereignty over, those (is)lands. *Terra nullius* was the wind on the sails of the storming *doctrine of discovery*, a political and legalized justification for the seizure of lands that were not inhabited by Christians. Colonialism and Christianity were partners in mapping (is)lands as empty and available for them to take over (cf. Havea 2018a). The Qur'an's declaration of open shore on the other hand

5. A Bush That Moved

acknowledges that the land might have been occupied but Jonah could land on it, if the native and traditional people of the land welcomed him.[1]

The Qur'an's assertion of open shore is the reverse of "closed border" policies in the current time that push "boat people" (read: refugees) away into the open sea or into detention centres where they are "processed" (like sardines).[2] The extreme of the closed border policies has provided justification for the erection of segregation walls by the modern state of Israel (against Palestine) and by the United States (against Mexico and Latin American nations to the south). On a different platform, but with racist sentiments through and through, the Brexit deal of the UK aims to close its borders with the neighbouring states of the European Union. The supremacist closed border policies of these modern and supposedly civilized nations, all of which have colonialist and religious legacies, are irrational and offensive in light of the Qur'an's open shore.

Jonah did not have to force himself ashore, but he may not have had a smooth landing. Allah "threw" him onto the shore. Several explanations of Allah's insensitive action are possible: the Qur'an echoes the biblical rhetoric of casting, hurling and throwing; Jonah might not have wanted to go there, so he had to be thrown ashore; Yнwн might have been frustrated (as expected, according to the biblical account) and uncaring.[3] Thwack! To make things worse for Jonah, he was ill when he was thrown onto the shore. Ouch! Notwithstanding, Allah was also compassionate. Allah caused a bush (gourd vine)[4] to grow over him to give him shade, shelter (one of the excuses for building detention centres for refugees) and the chance to regain his health and strength. At that Qur'anic narrative moment, Jonah was still at the open shore.

The Qur'an thus moved the bush, in both time and space. The bush came up at the open shore before Jonah goes to Nineveh, to shelter an ill voyager, instead of after Jonah came out of Nineveh, to shelter a dejected and judgemental messenger (see Chapter 3). Jonah's illness is understandable, having been swollen into a vessel

---

1. Muslim oral tradition resolves the issue of whether the native or traditional people welcomed Jonah by asserting that Jonah was sent to "his people."

2. In the case of Australia, the detention centres on Nauru and Papua New Guinea are known as the "Pacific solutions" to the Australian Commonwealth Government's fear of "invasion" by asylum seekers.

3. Because there are two canonical ends of the Jonah narrative in the Hebrew Bible and the Qur'an (see discussion at the end of Chapter 4), the exercise of *reading backward* takes both ends into account.

4. I opt to use "bush" (one of the translations for the Hebrew *qiqayon*, קיקיון) because it has significance for indigenous Australians, because it connotes weakness and worthlessness (as compared to vine) and because it instigates discrimination against the ancestors (as bush or *bushed*, meaning uncivilized, people). See further explanations offered in the chapter.

70 *Jonah*

(fish) in motion then thrown onto a hard and unmoving surface.[5] Jonah is vulnerable in the Qur'anic version (compared to the strong and almost superhero character in the Hebrew Bible who seemed to be physically and emotionally unaffected by his time and experience in the gut of the fish), and i imagine that some of his people would have felt sorry for him being ill, thrown and fishy.

Not only does the Qur'an provide a different image of Jonah, it also shifts assumptions about the bush and what took place around it. The bush is not burned, dried up or withered, and the Qur'an does not rule out the possibility that the bush could have grown bigger and stronger. The bush could also have flowered and bore fruits, as well as scattered seeds in the afterlife of the narrative. In this chapter i revisit the place of the bush in the narrative world of Jon. 4.1-9, beginning with the Qur'anic description of Jonah as one among those who exalt Allah (Sūrah 37.143, see also Chapter 6).

Among those who exalt

To deal with his displeasure and grief, according to the biblical account, Jonah resorted to prayer (פלל) in Jon. 4.1. This was not the only time he prayed, but on this occasion he exalted YHWH both in the popular sense of showing reverence and in the sense that Jonah paid tribute to and recognized YHWH as the one who was responsible for the impetus of his prayer. Jonah was in trouble, and he both revered and recognized YHWH *as the cause* of his trouble. The prayer was because of YHWH (as troublemaker), and it was also directed at YHWH (with hope that the trouble would stop). In revealing something about YHWH, the prayer *raised* (exalted) YHWH. At the same time, the prayer also revealed something about Jonah. I revisit Jon. 4.1-9 within this frame, reading it as two prayers: Jon. 4.1-4 and Jon. 4.5-9. While פלל (pray/er) is not used in Jon. 4.5-9, i take its positioning in relation to, and its shared structure with, Jon. 4.1-4, as well as the paralleling responses by YHWH (which links Jon. 4.1-4 with Jon. 4.5-9), as narrative invitations to read it as a prayer as well. I thus read Jon. 4.1-9 as two separable prayers rather than a two-part prayer.

There is a separation between the location of the first prayer (within the city) and the location of the second prayer (outside the city), and there is also a different mood in the two prayers: the narrator labels what Jonah did as פלל (pray; Jon. 4.2) in the first and as שאל (request, plea, supplication; Jon. 4.8b) in the second. The two prayers follow upon two very different events and experiences—the first follows the pardoning of Nineveh, and the second follows Jonah's fainting condition—but

---

5. Pasifika Islanders are familiar with many kinds of shores. Some shores are sandy, and one could land without a scratch; some shores are rocky, so one would be bruised but still survive; and some shores are cliffs, and one risks being thrown onto the seawall and drowning if one does not catch the right wave onto land. Which kind of shore he was thrown onto thus makes a difference.

5. A Bush That Moved

71

the request in both is the same: "[Take my life for] it is better that I die than live" (Jon. 4.3, 8). Though separate in both space and narrative frame, YHWH's responses (in Jon. 4.4 and Jon. 4.9a) link the two together. YHWH was under the impression that Jonah's prayer had something to do with Nineveh and the bush (rather than Jonah's condition), and why one (a wicked city) was spared but the other (an innocent plant) was destroyed. YHWH's explanation is straightforward: what happened to Nineveh and to the bush did not have to meet Jonah's approval. Jonah therefore had no right to grieve over YHWH's performance. Put sharply, it was none of his business.

Jon. 4.1-4

In the first prayer, Jonah began by complementing YHWH: "I know that you are a kind (חנן) God, as well as compassionate (רחם), far from anger, abundant in grace (חסד), and repenting (נחם) against evil" (Jon. 4.2b). The words of praise combine to make a strong voice of exaltation, and Jonah testifies that he had the same awareness while he was back in his own country (Jon. 4.2a). Jonah does not hold back, and he sounds sincere. The request that follows contradicts, on the surface, this exaltation. Not only did Jonah ask YHWH to let him die but on first reading he also dared YHWH to kill him: "Please, YHWH, take (לקח) my life (נפש) for it is better that I die than live" (Jon. 4.3). However, could Jonah have asked YHWH for something else other than to kill him off? While this question tempts one into the spheres of intentional fallacy, which could not be determined with any certainty, it opens up the text for reconsideration.

Under the influence of the Qur'anic characterization, i add here an alternative reading in which Jonah asked to be hassled rather than to be killed. This suggestion is based on Jonah's choice of words: first, the word לקח (take) in "take my life" connotes force and violence (e.g. the *taking* of Dinah by Shechem in Gen. 34.2 and of Bathsheba on behalf of David in 2 Sam. 11.4) but it does not necessarily mean termination of life. Second, the word נפש (translated as "life") also refers to breath and soul, in addition to referring to life in the physical, mortal sense. Because לקח could also be translated as "carry" (along) and "lead" (away), one could read Jonah's prayer as a request for care and respect: "Please, YHWH, *carry* or *lead* my soul" is not as lethal as "take my life" in the sense of "kill me" or "knock me off." On the basis of this alternative understanding, the second clause may be read in the comparative sense: Jonah asks YHWH to carry (לקח) his נפש because, at that time and place, death (which is yet to come) was better to him than living (read: what he was experiencing) at that point. Jonah was troubled, and he asked for care: "Please, YHWH, carry my soul for my future death is better than my current living." This is a reasonable and exalting request made to YHWH whom Jewish, Christian and Muslim traditions praise as the most compassionate, and the most merciful (cf. Qur'an 1.1).

This reading emphasizes the vulnerability of Jonah, a quality that comes through strongly in the Qur'anic version. Because YHWH had spared Nineveh, so Jonah requested the same for his own sake: "Please, YHWH, carry my soul for in my state of vulnerability my future death is better than my current living." And Yнwн responded with an open (rhetorical) question: "Is it good that you grieve?" (Jon. 4.4). In other words, grief emphasizes but does not relieve the susceptibility and despair of a vulnerable subject. In this reading, the tone of the exchange between Yнwн and Jonah shifts away from the tones of confrontation and antagonism. Jonah is vulnerable, and Yнwн is responsive (a different picture from the one i proposed in Chapter 3). Nonetheless, no resolution was reached in this first prayer. Yнwн was open-ended in Jon. 4.4 as in Jon. 4.10-11 (see Chapter 4).

This reading makes sense of locating Jonah's first prayer in Nineveh, within the hearing of the pardoned people of the land. Jonah was not antagonistic against Nineveh, his own people according to the Qur'an. His issue rather was with Yнwн, the most compassionate, the most merciful. Jonah did not hold back, and he prayed in the presence of a crowd of witnesses. He prayed that Yнwн extend the compassion given to Nineveh towards his own vulnerable body as well. Favouring the Qur'anic spirit (read: נפש), this alternative reading highlights Jonah's existential vulnerability.

The upshot of this reading is that it enables Jonah to subvert the assumption (which i proposed in Chapter 4) that the sparing of Nineveh was due to the action of the people and the beasts. In this reading, the sparing of Nineveh was not caused by anything other than Yнwн the most compassionate, the most merciful. In the hearing of the people of Nineveh, this first prayer exalted Yнwн and undermined any idea or expectation that they could change Yнwн's mind. In this regard, in this first prayer, Jonah begged to differ from his own people.

Jon. 4.5-9

The second prayer comes after Jonah is narratively pushed out of Nineveh. Interrupting the haste of the biblical narrative to move Jonah out of the city, the following reading slows the tempo into a prayer-like pace.

Away from the city, Jonah is exposed to the elements of the open space, especially the wind and the sun. He needed protection, and so he built a shelter (Jon. 4.5). With what? How long did it take?[6] Who knows! But Jonah did it, and he sat in his booth "until he sees what will be(come) in/with the city" (Jon. 4.5b). According to the *forward flow* of the narrative, when Jonah sat down under his booth he already knew that Nineveh repented and that Yнwн pardoned the city, so i do not expect him to be lurking to see if and when the city would be destroyed. That would require Yнwн to be uncompassionate, which contradicts the exaltation that Jonah had just given. If he was not expecting Nineveh to be destroyed, what else then was he waiting to see?

In Pasifika, when a village or family accomplishes a task there will be celebration with feasting and performances. Relatives and neighbouring communities are

---

6. Both questions are critical: the first question is critical given his outback context, and the second question is critical given his vulnerable condition.

5. A Bush That Moved

invited, and strangers who come through are invited to dally for the celebration. Could Jonah have been waiting for Nineveh to end the period of fasting and mourning so that the celebration may begin, and he would then go back to join (or crash) in their festivity? Could he have been waiting to see Nineveh reach the enjoyment that the Qur'an anticipated? Did Jonah know what to expect?

Even though the city is not named in Sūrah 37.147-8, the Qur'an presented Jonah as one who belonged to Nineveh. Without the control of the biblical narrative, the Qur'anic account suggests that he was sent to his people as part of the process for his recovery. He was ill, and he needed more care than what the bush at the shoreline could provide. Allah, the most compassionate, then sent him to his people, who numbered "a hundred thousand or more," that they might assist him in the healing process. In this reading, Jonah's body did not bring healing to Nineveh. Rather, his body needed healing from Nineveh. In this connection, "his people" prefigured the innkeeper in the so-called parable of the Good Samaritan (Lk. 10.25-37), the unnamed person who cared for the robbed man and trusted that the Samaritan would return and keep his words. The innkeeper is not considered in Jesus's question to his interlocutor—"Which of these three [Priest, Levite, Samaritan] do you think was a neighbor to the man who fell into the hands of the robbers" (Lk. 10.36)—or seen as "the one who had mercy" on the victim (Lk. 10.37).[7] In the intersection of the Qur'an's and Jesus's parable, Jonah was sent to his people for healing. The people believed without Jonah having to preach, and Allah gave them "enjoyment for a time."

Coming back to the biblical account and Jonah's booth, could Jonah be waiting to see what "enjoyment" means for Nineveh? That he went through the trouble to build a booth and then sat out in the hinterland suggest that he was serious with waiting to see what be(come) in/with the city. He could have gone back to his home ground (according to the biblical account), and let Nineveh go on with whatever they would do. But Jonah sat down, and waited.

Under his booth he was protected and he appeared to be somewhat secure. At some point later, as if in response to Jonah's first prayer, Yhwh showed Jonah some care. Yhwh provided the bush, which "grew up over Jonah, to provide shade for his head and save him from discomfort" (Jon. 4.6a). The process is narrated to give the impression that Yhwh threw a shawl or blanket over Jonah's head to give him added comfort (in addition to the shade he received from his booth), and Jonah appreciated Yhwh's care. In fact, he was very happy about the bush (Jon. 4.6b).

The biblical Jonah comes across to be as magical as Yhwh. Time seems to melt away as they performed their magic acts. Jonah built a booth out of thin air, and Yhwh responded with a bush that appeared instantly and fully grown. And then, on the next day, the worm joined the magic show. It ate the bush, and the bush withered. The sun and the wind came next, to finish the bush off as well as beat

---

7. The recent article by Mark A. Proctor misses this point, even though he followed Charles W. Hedrick's advice that "a parable will never speak in its own way as long as it is embedded in a literary context" (Proctor 2019: 204; citing Hedrick 2004: 90).

Jonah down on his head. When Jonah became faint, he "begged (שׁאל) his נפשׁ to die, saying that his death was better than his living" (Jon. 4.8b). Jonah's second prayer was with regard to his own condition, his faintness. He asked YHWH in his first prayer to "take his נפשׁ" (Jon. 4.3), and in his second prayer he "begged his נפשׁ to die" (Jon. 4.8). It appears that YHWH did not provide the care Jonah requested in the first prayer (as proposed above). At this point, Jonah was not at all concerned for the bush.

The turn to the bush came from the lips of YHWH: "Is it good, your grief for the bush?" (Jon. 4.9a). The question gives the impression that YHWH did not think much of the bush. It came up one day, and it was eaten the next day by a single worm.[8] The bush was a snack, it seems, not for two but only one worm. Why should Jonah grieve over an insignificant, dead bush? In shifting the focus to the bush's demise, YHWH refused to see the vulnerability of his messenger. In response, on first reading, Jonah turned from his own vulnerable condition to the fatal case of the bush: "My grief is good, even up to death" (Jon. 4.9b). The bush was worthy of Jonah's grief. Or in the youthful lingos of the current time, the bush was *to die for*. In this reading, Jonah went along with the diversion that YHWH introduced.

A second reading arises from the shift in the direction of the two prayers. YHWH still did not see Jonah's vulnerability (the impetus for his first prayer), and it makes sense that Jonah addressed his second prayer to a different subject—his נפשׁ (Jon. 4.8) instead of YHWH. He (after the first prayer) was done with YHWH. In this second reading Jonah remained resolute when YHWH tried to shift the focus to the bush. In the MT, Jonah does not say "Yes" (as in NRSV and NJPS) or indicate consent (as in NIV and NKJV) with YHWH. Jonah's resoluteness can be heard in the NASB translation:

Then God said to Jonah, "Do you have good reason to be angry about the plant?" And he said, "I have good reason to be angry, even to death." (Jon. 4.9)

Jonah did not give in to YHWH's attempt to shift attention to the bush. His focus remained with his grief (anger). In this reading, Jonah was resolute not because the bush was insignificant but because his vulnerable condition needed to be taken into account. His grief, which was caused by YHWH, was also significant.

The difference between the two readings raises the question of whether one sees Jonah (and oneself, as reader) giving in to YHWH's manipulation of the plot. The first reading sees Jonah going along with YHWH, while the second reading sees Jonah resisting YHWH. The first reading sees Jonah as one who is easily distracted, while the second sees in Jonah the courage to think differently. The first reading is more amen-able to an ecological reading, while the second reading embraces the נפשׁ of a messenger who had the courage to run away from the presence of, and

---

8. If the leaves were still green, this would make a good children's story: green leaves are healthier for a hungry or stomach-aching caterpillar.

5. A Bush That Moved

to push and talk back at, YHWH. Both readings are respectful of the text, and come together in Jon. 4.10-11 (see Chapter 4).

To die or not to die

Obviously, Jonah did not share YHWH's perspective. In seeing Jonah among "those who exalt Allah," i proposed as a first reading that the primary problem for Jonah was the way YHWH operated and how that impacted him as a person, on his vulnerable body (compared to him as a keeper of a tradition). YHWH cared for Nineveh but did not see the vulnerability of Jonah, and that was especially painful in the eyes of the Qur'an and Muslim oral tradition in which Jonah belonged to the people of Nineveh. In their eyes, YHWH was not compassionate to *all* of Nineveh. Because of that, i suggested that Jonah wanted out. He had enough of YHWH and did not want to be a part of his outfit any longer.[9]

The second reading is slightly nuanced, and it draws upon the first reading: Jonah did not want YHWH to hassle or kill him off, but invited YHWH to care for him instead. This is an alternative understanding of Jonah's demand for YHWH to "take my life" (read as "care for, carry, me"), with the next phrase taken as acknowledgement that his life was already so very bad that "it is better that I die than live." Jonah's prayer was not a death wish, but a request for care: "Carry me, for at this point my dying is better than my living."

Both readings circle around Nineveh, and YHWH brought the bush into the picture by suggesting (in the second prayer) that Jonah wanted to die also because of the bush. For YHWH, the bush was disposable. To the contrary, the above readings suggested that YHWH's view irritated Jonah and he wanted YHWH to value the bush and not brush it off as if it was not significant; the bush (the subject of the second prayer) was as significant as the humans (the subject of the first prayer). This suggestion takes advantage of the separation between the two prayers and assumes that Jonah's anxiety and impetus differ between the two prayers. Thus, in the second prayer Jonah exalted YHWH in a critical way—by pointing out that the bush was worth dying for:

> But God said to Jonah, "Is it right for you to be angry about the bush?" And he said, "Yes, angry enough to die." (Jon. 4.9, NRSV)

The bush was attacked and it withered (Jon. 4.8). If as a consequence the bush died in front of Jonah, Jonah would have seen in its death the release that dying provides for a withered body. (The bush would have been among the characters that died at the background of the narrative.) If the bush withered but did not die before Jonah offered his prayer, Jonah would have seen his own vulnerability in the bush. In

---

9. In this first reading, Jonah's feeling about YHWH has not shifted since the opening verses of the book.

76   *Jonah*

both cases, the condition of the bush shaped Jonah's prayers. In other words, the bush *moved* Jonah.

Ancestors and children in the bush

I recall here the overturning of conventional thinking about roots and leaves in the artworks by the late West Papuan activist Donatus Moiwend (aka Donet, discussed in Chapter 1). For Donet, the leaves represent the ancestors because leaves have voices and they give air for breathing and sap for healing, while the roots represent the children (future generation) because new life starts from the roots and the roots ground and feed the plant (as children do for parents in the old age). Both the leaves and the roots play important roles in sustaining the plant, and the health of one is visible in the other.[10]

The plant in Jonah's story is not a tree with strong branches, but a bush (קיקיון, *qiqayon*). According to general scholarly consensus, קיקיון is a gourd with large leaves and it grows like a vine with a lot of leaves and roots. Following Donet's thinking, קיקיון brings alive the strong connection between the ancestors and the next generation (children). As a vine the קיקיון does not have a trunk and so Donet's metaphor is humbling for the current generation (parents): we are not very strong or steady. Returning to Jonah's second prayer, there is no separation between a human person (first prayer) and caring for a קיקיון (second prayer). On account of Donet's West Papuan wisdom, the two prayers could be interwoven or, like the roots beaten as drums in the rainforests of Papua and the Solomon Islands, the two prayers communicate with each other (as they do in the narrative). Compassion for Nineveh does not exclude caring for (manifest in the capacity to grieve over) the קיקיון and (owing to the Qur'an text) caring for a vulnerable individual.[11]

As indicated above, i prefer "bush" as translation for קיקיון and i have three main reasons for this option. First, because the term "bush" has special connotations for indigenous Australian colleagues—they speak with pride about being "bush people" (even though many of them grew up in cities and urban areas) and the ceremonies that take place while "going bush." The so-called secret business ceremonies (some for men and some for women) that they hold while "going bush" shape indigenous identity and channel indigenous wisdom to the next generation. The bush is not an empty or menacing space for these indigenous Australians but a place of initiation, pilgrimage, formation and learning.[12] I see the

---

10. While leaves are more visible, in the rainforests of Papua and the Solomon Islands, the roots of giant trees pop up like vines above the ground and people communicate by beating the roots like drums. In this way, roots have voices in the bush (forest).

11. In the assertion made here, the *reading backward* approach encourages and enables the intersecting of biblical, Qur'anic and West Papuan texts.

12. Because of urbanization, some of the ceremonies take place at "bush" places close to towns and cities.

same in the case of Jonah: the bush was a place for learning—to see what becomes in the city—initiation and formation (in his prayers).

Second, i use "bush" in order to expose and subvert the assumption that a bush (shrub) is not significant because it is not big or strong. The value of a bush is not in its size or strength but, to borrow from the "burning bush" experience of Moses even though a different word is used in his story (סנה in Exod. 3.2-3 may have been a pun on the name Sinai, סיני in Exod. 19.18), in what it reveals and connotes. In the Jonah narrative, the bush connotes additional protection and comfort which, for a vulnerable body, was valuable and appreciated.

And third, i use "bush" in order to call attention to the disguised association of the ancestors with, as people of, the bush (jungle). This association results in discrimination against the ancestors as uncivilized bush people. In this connection, the process of *reading backward* (in terms of direction) is intentional about engaging the wisdom and civilization of subjects who are ignored or pushed aside because they are seen as "backward." Since one of the popular readings of Jon. 4.1-9 finds Jonah to be antagonistic against YHWH, he is easily slotted a place among the "backward characters" or the mob of "bushmen." In accounting for the Qur'an text and the vulnerability of Jonah, the readings proposed above find meaning in the body, words and character of Jonah.

Those explanations, under the influence of native and indigenous wisdom, push readers to consider what Jonah might have sat down to see be(come) in the city. I cannot rule out the possibility that Jonah built a shelter (סכה)[13] and waited to see how the next generation (roots) of Nineveh turn out. It does not matter in the narrative if Jonah had a mat to sit on or not, but it makes a difference that he was sheltered and comfortable. If he sat down to see what would become of the next generation in Nineveh, then he was there for longer than most readers allow.

The moves in my *reading backward* process, however, do not account for one of the responses i received when i presented Donet's thoughts at a conference at Christchurch, New Zealand (October 2, 2018). At the end of the presentation, i received an anonymous note with a critical question in *Haiku* structure:

> If children are roots
> What stops those of us with none
> from flying away?

This is one of those questions that says a lot. Many people do not have children, and it might insult them if i were to suggest fostering or adopting the children of

---

13. Whether one translates סכה—the structure that Jonah built—as "booth" or "shelter" suggests the length of time that one imagines Jonah planned to spend there. The difference between "booth" (which suggests temporary stay) and "shelter" (which suggests extended dwelling) might be significant for city folk, but not in the same way for native and indigenous people. What matters for native and indigenous people is protection, hence my use of "shelter."

78   *Jonah*

others as a way of taking roots. The question, nonetheless, keeps the attention on subjects in Nineveh who are ignored in the narrative, among whom are many children and youth, and by many readers. Those ignored subjects did not deserve to be annihilated along with the city, and i imagine that they would have appreciated if the reason why Jonah sat down was to see what would become of and for them. Jonah was concerned because they too were vulnerable.

From the bush to Nineveh

Reading Jon. 4.1-9 backward in the spirit of the Qur'an version presents alternative views. In addition to the link that YHWH made in his responses to Jonah's prayers, two other links may be drawn between the bush and Nineveh. First, the city in the Qur'an is not as wicked as YHWH presented it in the biblical narrative. The negative attitudes against Nineveh in many circles are out of concern for the "Pride of Jacob" and the "Pride of Israel" (Nah. 2.3a). The humiliating and ruthless devastation announced against Nineveh in the book of Nahum (e.g. Nah. 3.5b—"I will lift up your skirts over your face and display your nakedness to the nations and your shame to the kingdoms") is not found in the Jonah narrative. As it is unfair to privilege Nahum's agenda in one's reading of the characterization of Nineveh in the Jonah narrative, so it is unfair to privilege YHWH's bias in the book of Jonah over against other biases in the same text. Nahum represents one voice in the Bible, as does YHWH in the Jonah narrative. Concerning Nineveh, there are other voices in the Bible, other voices in the Jonah narrative and other voices in other scriptures, and hearing those voices in juxtaposition makes for a richer reading.

Other factors that contribute to the demonizing of Nineveh are the anti-city and anti-urban biases in biblical literature, which are found back in the stories of Cain as the city founder (Gen. 4.17) and the builders of the tower at Babel (Gen. 11.1-9). The biblical narrator does not approve of those cities mainly because they are against the preferred nomadic lifestyle for the wandering ancestors of Judah and Israel. As a city, Nineveh was by default associated with wickedness, similar to the way that Sodom and Gomorrah also received a bad rap in many circles. Juxtaposing the biblical and the Qur'anic texts on Jonah proves that those biases do not do justice to Nineveh as a textual and historical city. Nineveh is not wicked, ignorant, naive or simple (contra Jon. 4.11). Nineveh is not just any city, but a location with people and animals.

Second, in light of the Qur'anic version, Nineveh is not a city in grief or one that needs to be pardoned. Rather, Nineveh is a people that believed and that received the gift of and the space for enjoyment. This is a very different picture from what the book of Nahum paints, but it is a picture that one could read in the book of Jonah if, as suggested above, one does not privilege the biased views of YHWH.

In Jon. 4.1-8 YHWH turned from Nineveh to Jonah but did not see his vulnerability, and then proceeded to brush Jonah off along with the bush. Against YHWH's drive, i suggested previously that Jonah cared for the bush and i emphasize here that Jonah cared for Nineveh as well. This insight brings me back to the beginning of the pericope: Jonah sat down and waited to "see what be(come) in or with the city" (Jon. 4.5b). Against readings which assume that Jonah was waiting to see the city being destroyed, which is supposed to be what he wanted, i suggest that Jonah was waiting to see if YHWH will let the city be(come). Jonah sat down with no plan of going anywhere for a while, to see that YHWH comes through in being the most compassionate, and the most merciful, towards Nineveh. He sat down to see that YHWH will spare Nineveh. In this reading Jonah did not fully trust YHWH, and what happened to the bush supported his distrust.

Jonah was thus a good match for YHWH. As suggested in Chapter 3, YHWH's drive was to see if Jonah would collaborate (come under the divine shadow), and in this reading Jonah sat down to see if YHWH would come clean (read: if YHWH would come into the shades of his booth and the shelter of his bush). This reading does not link the bush and the city according to their status in YHWH's eyes (a wicked city and a dead bush) but according to the experience of a vulnerable Jonah: he wanted to see (read: assure) that the city receives comfort and enjoyment, as he had received from the bush.

Chapter 6

A CITY THAT BELIEVED (JON. 3.1-10)

Upon hearing Jonah's proclamation (Jon. 3.4) the people of Nineveh believed אלהים (God), and they performed rituals that are usually associated with grief and repentance (Jon. 3.5). What the city believed and repented worked wonder-fully on אלהים: "When אלהים saw what they did, that they turned from their evil ways, אלהים relented the evil which he said to do to them—he did not do it" (Jon. 3.10). The city believed and repented, and as a consequence it inspired אלהים to also repent. However, the text does not specify if the אלהים that the city believed was the God of the Hebrews (cf. Jon. 1.9) and the narrator or the God of the city (Jon. 3.3 in the Hebrew Bible identifies Nineveh as a "city of God"). The text teases the imaginations and biases of readers with both possibilities.

Jonah 3 brings the topic of compassion (my emphasis in Chapter 5) into the shadows of repentance, and i continue *reading backward* in this chapter by unpacking both topics *with respect* to the city of Nineveh. While the city is the primary subject of interest in my revisit of Jon. 3.1-10 in this chapter, the city occasionally gets lost in my engagement with the theological and cultural baggage of the text. I am thus obliged to stress early in this chapter that the interest of the city (as space, as construction and as people) is my primary concern, but i shall not repeat my argument for the city as an *earthed subject* (see Chapter 3).

Compassion and repentance

In the eyes of the city of Nineveh, Yhwh became the "most compassionate" (cf. Qur'an 1.1) because he repented—compassion and repentance intersect. In this claim, repentance is a (but not the only) condition for compassion. The humility to repent encourages and facilitates compassion but repentance will not automatically result in compassion.

My claim requires taking into account the capacity to repent when one deals with or dwells on the compassion of Yhwh; in the case of Nineveh, Yhwh the most compassionate was a repentant one. This does not mean that Yhwh is always or consistently compassionate and repentant. Notwithstanding, my claim affirms that repentance is not a flaw in the character of Yhwh, nor in the case of other

6. A City That Believed 81

repentant characters such as the Ninevites in the Jonah narrative, and anticipates two critical questions: Could Yʜwʜ be compassionate without also, or first, being repentant? And from the other direction, could Yʜwʜ be repentant without also being compassionate? These questions lurk behind the *return to* Jonah 3.1-10 in this chapter with the expectation that, since repentance involves "turning" and "returning," some of the observations concerning the text in this chapter might *repent* readings proposed in previous pages.[1]

The two questions that i anticipate are critical from faith and theological standpoints because they go against biblical theologies that take, first, the God/Yʜwʜ-*character* in biblical texts to be one and the same as the God-*being* in faith and Christian imaginations and second, God's mercy and grace (two words for "compassion") as gifts which are freely given and thus unconditional. The first reflects the monotheistic illusion of Christian faith and theologies, and the second reflects, in my Methodist heritage, the concept of prevenient grace which proclaims that God's mercy precedes human decisions and it is not to be mixed up with the concept of charity. God's mercy is open and unconditional, the outpouring of God's benevolence; whereas charity is God's response to life struggles and it is therefore reserved and directed, and conditioned by something external to God (and in the case of charitable humans). Traditional biblical theologies thus conceive Yʜwʜ as a sovereign God that is unaffected, as both a transcendent (as in Genesis 1 and Jonah 1) and an immanent (as in Genesis 2–3 and Jonah 3–4) character. In the reading suggested in Chapter 4, to the contrary, the beasts open up Yʜwʜ's mercy for negotiation. In the eyes of Nineveh and its beasts, Yʜwʜ was open to being influenced and to being conditioned. Yʜwʜ was repent-able.

The two anticipated questions are critical from hermeneutical standpoints as well because they defy the favouring of Yʜwʜ (as literary character) by biblical narrators and by a host of readers. In the Bible, Yʜwʜ could get away with almost anything he does including the raining of destruction upon earth (e.g. in the Genesis flood narrative) as well as the sanctioning of dispersion (e.g. Babel story), invasion, occupation and genocide (e.g. of Canaan-Palestine in the books of Joshua and Judges). In principle, Yʜwʜ is a biblical character who is by default untouchable by readers.

On the other hand, textual references that present Yʜwʜ as one who repented show that he, on some occasions, was affected by what happened around and before him, and that he could change his mind and his ways. Yʜwʜ was sometimes sorry for his evil plans and wicked acts. Following this line, i *return to* Jon. 3.1-10 in this chapter with the assumption that the capacity and humility to repent enabled Yʜwʜ to become the most compassionate, at least in the case of Nineveh.

---

1. It is expected that *reading backward* (similar to the benefit of seeing things in hindsight) may make one change one's mind (the stuff of repentance).

82   *Jonah*

Among those who repent

The repentance of Yhwh is not a comfortable subject for many readers primarily because that attribute presents Yhwh as one who was wrong, and who accepted being wrong, but this subject is not foreign or strange in the biblical memory. As a literary character who crosses over several biblical narratives, generations and timelines, Yhwh is remembered as one who occasionally accepted that he was wrong and who consequently could repent.

In the flood narrative (Genesis 6–9) Yhwh repented both prior to and after the flood, but for different reasons. Before the flood, Yhwh repented for something he had done. Yhwh was sorry to have made humans because every plan they devised turned out to be "nothing but evil all the time. And the Lord regretted that He had made man on earth, and His heart was saddened" (Gen. 6.5b-6, NJPS). The buck stopped with Yhwh. As a consequence, Yhwh decided to wipe out humans *together with* beasts (*b'hemah*), creeping things and birds. Prior to the flood, Yhwh's repentance resulted in destruction rather than compassion. Instead of correcting his mistake, Yhwh opted to destroy the evidence. The flood was Yhwh's *wipe out* device. The narrative does not explain why the animals were also wiped out, whether or not they had anything to do with the alleged evil plans of humans. The animals appear to be victims of the human's evil device along with innocent children (cf. Fewell 2003) and youth whose victimization—hinted after the flood, "Never again will I doom the earth because of man, since the devisings of man's mind are evil *from his youth*" (Gen. 8.21b, NJPS; my italics)—counts among the atrocious acts of ecological injustice.

The narrative is silent about the substance of the humans' plans. What was so evil to warrant the flood? The previous pericope (Gen. 6.1-5) narrates border crossing and sexual encounters: the humans had daughters who were "good" (טוב; translated as "fair" in several translations, which suggests biases concerning complexion) and they were taken (לקח) by the sons of God. The narrative does not explain if the daughters consented or if their parents gave their blessing or permission. Did the sons of God rape the goodly human daughters?

The daughters produced children for the sons of God, and the narrative locates these encounters at the time of the Nephilim. Human daughters could produce babies, but the narrative does not present the humans as thinking or conspiratorial beings. The humans in Gen. 6.1-5 are presented as passive and who may have been overpowered. The characters who had "dirty" thoughts and who committed aggressive actions were the sons of God. In this context, the narrator pulls a fast one by expecting readers to accept the allegation that the plans of humans were evil *all the time*! This *reading backward* to Gen. 6.1-5 invites suspicion over the differentiation between plans (of humans) and actions (of sons of God and of Yhwh). The humans are accused of having evil plans, but the narrative does not judge Yhwh for his deadly action (flooding earth). Accepting the gravity of the latter is an opportunity for repentance, a humbling exercise in self-critique.

After the flood, Yhwh showed remorse: "Never again will I doom the earth because of man, since the devisings of man's mind are evil from his youth; *nor will*

I ever again destroy every living being, as I have done" (Gen. 8.21b, NJPS; my italics). A Hebrew word that may be translated as "repentance" is not used in YHWH's expression of remorse after the flood, but the kindred of the *before and after* frames of the narrative gives a repentant tone to YHWH's admission. This is emphasized by YHWH's commitment to not cause a flood again (Gen. 9.11) in the context of cutting a covenant (Gen. 9.9-17). The flow of the narrative into the covenant ritual after the flood, the primary aim of which is to remind YHWH *not to do it again*, gives the impression of remorse and repentance.

Before the flood, YHWH repented of something that he had done—that he made humans. This repentance led to destruction. After the flood, YHWH repented of something else that he had done—that he destroyed every living being. YHWH's repentance after the flood resulted from compassion towards the victims of his previous repentance. However, YHWH's compassion could not help the drowned victims of the flood. And lest we are drowned by the emphasis of this reflection on the repentance of YHWH, it should be repeated that the flood was an ecological disaster. Humans were not the only victims, and this is highlighted in the post-flood covenant that YHWH made with Noah and his seeds (Gen. 9.9) "and every living creature of all flesh that is upon the earth" (Gen. 9.16). While plants are not covenanted, YHWH's compassion extends to "all flesh upon the earth" in the second instance of repentance.

In Saul's story, YHWH also repented of something that he had done: "I regret that I made Saul king, for he has turned away from Me and has not carried out My commands" (1 Sam. 15.11, NJPS). Like the humans prior to the flood, Saul is rejected for turning away from YHWH. Whether Saul failed or was set up to fail is open for interpretation (see Gunn 1980), but that YHWH repented is clear from the text. YHWH did something which he later saw to be wrong, and he regretted having done so. Whereas YHWH's second repentance in the flood narrative led to compassion, there was no compassion for Saul. In this connection, there is no guarantee that repentance will *result* in compassion. This admission does not undermine the suggestion that repentance is a *condition* (but not a guarantee) for compassion. The different consequences of repentance, before and after the flood and in the story of Saul, witness to the complexity of the subject of repentance in the Bible.

YHWH's repentance in the golden calf narrative (Exodus 32) is different in orientation, because in this case YHWH repented of evil that he had *planned* against his own people. Moses was the main cause of the situation. He had gone up the mountain to consult with YHWH and was delayed in returning to the camp, so the people were anxious and asked his own brother and spokesperson Aaron (see Exod. 4.10-17) to make gods to go before them. The people had given up on Moses, and Aaron was eager to step up. Aaron gave instructions and the people quickly delivered. They collected and gave their gold rings to Aaron, who moulded the gold into the form of a calf and the people declared, "These are your gods, O Israel, who brought you up out of the land of Egypt!" (Exod. 32.4b). The next day, the people offered sacrifices then sat down to eat and drink, then they stood up to revel.[2] These actions angered Y{\sc hwh} to the point that he wanted his wrath to burn hot so that he could consume them (Exod. 32.10). For the sake of the people, Moses (who did not know the role of his spokesperson and representative brother in what happened in the camp) stepped in:

> But Moses implored the L{\sc ord} his God, and said, "O L{\sc ord}, why does your wrath burn hot against your people, whom you brought out of the land of Egypt with great power and with a mighty hand? Why should the Egyptians say, 'It was with evil intent that he brought them out to kill them in the mountains, and to consume them from the face of the earth'? Turn from your fierce wrath; change your mind and do not bring disaster on your people. Remember Abraham, Isaac, and Israel, your servants, how you swore to them by your own self, saying to them, 'I will multiply your descendants like the stars of heaven, and all this land that I have promised I will give to your descendants, and they shall inherit it forever.'" *And the L{\sc ord} changed his mind about the disaster that he planned to bring on his people.* (Exod. 32.11-14, NRSV; my italics)

Moses spoke on behalf of Israel, and this caused Y{\sc hwh} to change his mind and repent from what he had planned. Israel benefited from a mediator, but there is a twist of irony in the narrative: at that point, the mediator did not know that Israel had given up on and turned away from him. Moses negotiated for a people who had moved away from him. As a condemned people, it helped that a mediator negotiated for Israel. This privilege was not available in the flood and Saul narratives. Noah was not in any relationship with, and he did not negotiate on behalf of, the rest of humanity, and Samuel was against Saul from the beginning of his reign as king.[3]

The repentance of Y{\sc hwh} in the golden calf narrative prefigures his repentance in the Jonah narrative in the sense that Y{\sc hwh} repented of evil *planned* against a people. A key difference between the two narratives is that the people in Exodus 32 were the elected and covenanted people of Y{\sc hwh}, whereas the people of Nineveh were not. Or could Y{\sc hwh}'s repentance and compassion towards Nineveh be (read as) evidence that the people of Nineveh thereby *became* Y{\sc hwh}'s people? This question points to other points of differences between the two narratives: Israel (people of God) turned away from Moses and from Y{\sc hwh} (given that the people referred to the golden calf as the gods who brought them out of Egypt) whereas Nineveh turned to Y{\sc hwh}. Y{\sc hwh}'s compassion in the wilderness was for the sake of his reputation and prior commitments, compared to Y{\sc hwh}'s compassion for

---

2. A contrapuntal reading is possible here: whereas the revelling of Israel contributed towards angering Y{\sc hwh}, the repentance of Y{\sc hwh} resulted in the enjoyment of Nineveh.

3. Juxtaposing the character of Saul with the character of Nineveh, Samuel comes across as a prefigure for Jonah who, in traditional understanding, was against the sparing of Nineveh (compare to the reading proposed in Chapter 5, according to which Jonah was concerned for Nineveh).

Nineveh which was inspired by a believing and transformed people. Moses mediated for Israel; Nineveh mediated for themselves. In the Jonah narrative, repentance is a condition for Yhwh's compassion towards (seen in the pardoning of) Nineveh. This is not to say (in response to the claim and questions raised above) that repentance always results in compassion. Rather, the stress of this reflection is that repentance indicates openness and *affection* (even though Yhwh is not consistent on both counts).

The view that i favour in this reflection differs from Jonah's. According to Jonah (as a character), Yhwh's compassionate nature, which is understood to be all about Yhwh and nothing about Nineveh, is the condition for the pardoning of Nineveh (Jon. 4.1-9; see Chapter 5). The narrative, as read here, does not share Jonah's position. Yhwh's compassion results from Yhwh's repentance, which was in response to the people and animals of Nineveh (see Chapter 4). Ironically, Jonah expected Yhwh to be capable of repenting. In pushing Yhwh to change his mind and his ways concerning Nineveh (in Jonah 3) as well as concerning himself (in Jonah 4), Jonah affirmed that Yhwh could repent (as change of mind, heart and ways).

With respect to the person of Jonah, on the other hand, Yhwh is not repentant. Yhwh insisted twice that Jonah goes to Nineveh, and twice Yhwh refused to let Jonah die. The former suggests that Yhwh was serious about his word reaching Nineveh (a query raised in Chapter 2), and the two instances together show that Yhwh is not a pushover. Yhwh is capable of repenting, but *not all the time*. There is no assurance when Yhwh will repent and on what grounds. In the case of Yhwh, the matter of repentance is indeterminate.

Though the orientations of Yhwh's repentance differ in the narratives discussed herein, together these narratives unambiguously locate Yhwh among those who repent. The difference that the Nineveh narrative brings is the problematizing of Israel as a people having exclusive privilege to Yhwh's compassion. In the Jonah narrative, Yhwh's repentance and compassion locate Nineveh among the people who are favoured by Yhwh. This view allows for considering Jonah *as a mediator* for Nineveh, his own people (according to the Qur'an), as Moses mediated for Israel in the wilderness.

Fakatomala

The Tongan word for "repentance" is *fakatomala*, which is constructed with two words: *fakatō* (drop, remove, release) and *mala* (burden, disaster, misfortune). This Tongan term suggests that repentance is a procedure or ritual that aims to remove a burden.

Repentance (*fakatomala*) presupposes some kind of relationship (the Tongan word for which is *vā*, see Ka'ili 2005) and expects that the subjects in the relationship are affected by what is being repented as well as by the act of repentance. One performs *fakatomala* upon oneself—i repent of an action that i have done or plan to do; and one performs *fakatomala* on behalf of subjects with whom one relates—i perform *fakatomala* in order to drop (or lift) the burden that

86   *Jonah*

weigh down upon my relations. Correspondingly, my burdens are lifted when my relations perform *fakatomala*. As repentance, *fakatomala* is relational as well as reciprocal. Because one is in and opts to keep one's *vā* (relationship), one is obliged to *fakatomala*.

Subjects in a relationship do not have the same abilities and gifts because some are more ambitious and aggressive than others. When relations are disrupted or broken, *fakatomala* is needed in order to reestablish the relationship. In those situations, *fakatomala* is not about compassion (feeling sorry and affection for another) but about one's role and responsibility to one's relations and relatives. Returning to the focus of this study, how might the relational and reciprocal aspects of *fakatomala* impact the review of Yhwh's repentance in the Nineveh narrative?

Since *fakatomala* takes place in the context of a relationship in which subjects are obliged to one another and they as a consequence reciprocate, this procedure or ritual draws attention to the hidden elements of power in the biblical understandings of repentance and compassion. In all of the narratives of repentance discussed in the previous section, Yhwh was in a position of power from which he repented. Yhwh repented after destroying the world with the flood, after Saul challenged his and Samuel's authorities and after he planned to exercise his power by destroying Israel and Nineveh. At the bottom of Yhwh's repentance are clues of his power and authority, but these clues are under-read or read-over in part because Yhwh is considered to be untouchable. Whereas the review in the previous section linked Yhwh's repentance to compassion, the *fakatomala* frame orients repentance towards power—Yhwh's repentance (*fakatomala*) exposes his power. Yhwh would not have had to repent if he did not have the power to plan and do terrible things. And by extension, the compassion that Yhwh extended to the creation, Israel and Nineveh, are exercises of his power. In this configuration, repentance and compassion expose as well as put a check on Yhwh's power.

The discussions in the previous section focused on the repentance of Yhwh, but other characters also repented in Jon. 3.1-10. The words of Jonah had an immediate impact on the people: they "believed (אמן) in God, and they proclaimed a fast, great and small alike put on sackcloth" (Jon. 3.5). The people believed, they were convinced, but the narrator does not indicate if they also repented, or *turned* from their ways. It is only when the king joined the people and gave his decree that the rhetoric of repentance comes into the narrative: "Let everyone turn back (שוב, Qal imperfect) from his evil ways and from the injustice from which he is guilty" (Jon. 3.8b). Trusting the narrator and God—"God saw what they did, how they were turned (שוב, Qal perfect) back from their evil ways" (Jon. 3.10a)—i assume that the people went along with their king. The king played the role of mediator but, unlike Moses in Exodus 32, he appealed to the people. The king was obliged to the people, and so were the people to the king—their relationship enabled *fakatomala*. And it worked, for the people *were turned back* from their evil ways (so NJPS) and that was a condition for Yhwh responding with his own repentance and compassion. Intersecting Jonah 3 with Exodus 32 finds the people of Nineveh at a place of power. Similar to Yhwh in Exodus 32, the people of Nineveh turned from their evil ways.

The turning (repentance) of Nineveh *removed burden* (literal meaning of *fakatomala*) from upon Yhwh. In other words, the people of Nineveh helped Yhwh out. This suggestion could be read in two ways: that the people of Nineveh lightened Yhwh's burden, and that the people of Nineveh enlightened Yhwh's way (by lifting his anger). This twin suggestion is affirming of the people of Nineveh as a figure for "people of the land." In Jonah 3, the people of Nineveh are natives (or indigenous people) who (en)lightened Yhwh. In other words, borrowing from the Qur'an, the people gave Yhwh enjoyment.

I stress the connection between the city folk of Nineveh and natives because both—the people of Nineveh as city folk and as people with Assyrian heritage, and the native people (indigenous, people of the land, bush people) everywhere—do not often receive the attention and compassion of readers. Stressing the connection between the people of Nineveh and the native people is my attempt to inspire *fakatomala* among readers on behalf of both. Doing so would be respectful of Yhwh, who had no qualm about repenting on behalf of Nineveh (as the native people in the world of the Jonah narrative).

Seriously

One of the questions that i raised in Chapter 3 is whether Yhwh was serious about his words reaching Nineveh and consequently about overthrowing Nineveh. The people and king of Nineveh believed that Yhwh was serious, and they changed their ways and ended up (en)lightening Yhwh. This, however, does not make sense of why Yhwh made no fuss but almost instantly "repented (נחם) the evil he planned to do to them, and did not do it" (Jon. 3.10b). Yhwh's response was quick and easy, hence my query: What if in the first instance Yhwh was not serious about punishing Nineveh? This question cannot be answered with any certainty, of course, so the reflections that follow circle around the realms of possibility.

The reflection on Yhwh's repentance shows that Yhwh cannot be fixed to one mood or to a rigid frame of mind. Yhwh was flexible and changeable with respect to Nineveh. He was conditioned, moved to change. On the other hand, in the case of Jonah, Yhwh was static and rigid. He did not budge; he did not move. In this connection, Yhwh can be deadly serious as well as not too serious. I take this complication as providing the possibility that, in the Jonah narrative, Yhwh could be serious as well as be fooling around with Nineveh (see Jagessar 2018) and has thus tricked many readers (see Havea and Melanchthon 2016). It is the possibility that Yhwh was not completely serious, but fooling around with Nineveh, that consumes me in the following reflections.

Nineveh, as many readers have concluded, is outside of Yhwh's jurisdiction. If Yhwh were to overthrow Nineveh, that would count as an invasion (see also Dube 1998). While invasion is not novel to Yhwh, who previously sanctioned and enabled the invasion of other lands and homes (including in the wilderness)

88   *Jonah*

outside of his jurisdiction, the no-fuss way with which Yʜᴡʜ repented from invading Nineveh makes me pause. Reading Jon. 3.1-10 as the "Nineveh narrative" gives it a different feel compared to the wilderness and Canaanite narratives. So i wonder if Yʜᴡʜ has learnt something from his previous bloody invasions. (And if so, then good on him!)

Reading backward, the Nineveh narrative could be read as a critique of the narratives of liberation (in Exodus and Numbers) and occupation (in Joshua and Judges). Perspectives and biases make a difference here because the narratives of liberation and occupation favour the Israelites, compared to the people of Nineveh who won Yʜᴡʜ's compassion in Jonah 3. Nineveh was not passive, and the king of Nineveh was able to do what the kings of Moab (see Numbers 22–4) and Jericho (see Joshua 2) could not do namely,[4] he saved his city and people. In reading Jonah 3 as Nineveh's story we uncover the proverbial elephant in readings of the Jonah narrative, vis-à-vis Israel. The narrative does not name nor make any references to Israel. The Jonah narrative is not about or for Israel. Putting Israel to the side, my queries become more pertinent: What if Yʜᴡʜ was fooling around with Nineveh? If Yʜᴡʜ was not serious about overthrowing Nineveh, then for what was Nineveh a foil? Was Yʜᴡʜ using Nineveh to get at Jonah?

In this process of reading backward (without the influence of Jonah 1), Yʜᴡʜ's instruction in Jon. 3.2 is key: "Arise, go to Nineveh that great city and proclaim to it the proclamation that I tell you." The narrator quickly explained that Jonah arose and went as Yʜᴡʜ told him (Jon. 3.3a) but he did not reveal (and he may not have known) what the content of Yʜᴡʜ's proclamation was, and readers tend to trust Jonah, that what he proclaimed is actually what Yʜᴡʜ told him: "Forty days more, and Nineveh shall be overthrown" (Jon. 3.4b). However, in light of the reading proposed in Chapter 5 that Jonah was vulnerable, i raise here the possibility that Yʜᴡʜ's proclamation (signalled in Jon. 3.2b) was not the same as Jonah's proclamation (revealed in Jon. 3.4b). In other words, i wonder if Yʜᴡʜ gave a proclamation that Jonah could not stomach so he reframed Yʜᴡʜ's proclamation in order to save his own face. This suggestion keeps Jonah on a different page from Yʜᴡʜ, and there are hints of the possible dissonance within the narrative itself.

First, while Yʜᴡʜ's command has two elements—first the command to go, and second the undisclosed proclamation that he was to deliver—which were announced in one breath (Jon. 3.2), these are separated in the narrative (Jon. 3.3a and 3.4b). In between the two elements, the narrator explained that Jonah walked for one day (Jon. 3.4a). Jonah went but he delayed making the proclamation for one day, which is a long stretch of time for pondering and reconsideration. The separation of the two elements, which is understandable in terms of the account because Jonah had to set off on the journey and deliver the proclamation after he reached his targeted audience, raises suspicion. Why did the narrator insert the detail in Jon. 3.4a that Jonah walked for a day before he started to deliver his

---

4. Similar to the Pharaohs of Egypt in the exodus and wilderness narratives, these characters are not named as persons but presented as heads of empires.

proclamation? Was the narrator, who is careful with details, trying to say something by separating these two elements and delaying the proclamation? Because of the separation and postponement, one can be certain that Jonah's going was in obedience to Yнwн's command but cannot also be certain concerning the proclamation that he delivered. The narrator could have removed any suspicions with one stroke—"Jonah went at once to Nineveh *and delivered the proclamation in accordance with the* Lord's *command*" (modifying NJPS rendering of Jon. 3.3a; my italics).

Second, Jonah's delay in delivering the proclamation until he was one day into the city (Jon. 3.4) also raises suspicions. I suggested in Chapter 3 that the delay may have been due to class biases on the part of Jonah, given that the people at the fringes of the city were most likely lower- and working-class people. Here i add the possibility that Jonah was not cozy with Yнwн's proclamation and he took a day to figure out what to say instead. Jonah was quick to get up and go, but he hesitated to speak out. This puts Jonah in the company of Moses, who initially did not accept the mission that Yнwн gave him (see Exod. 4.1-17), and Ezekiel, for whom Yнwн's words were offensive (see Ezekiel 4). Moreover, but for a different reason, this puts Jonah in the shadows of Saul, whom Samuel accused of not carrying out the instructions of Yнwн (1 Sam. 15.11). These juxtapositions allow for the possibility that Jonah too was troubled, as those other key biblical characters were, by the words of Yнwн. The words of Yнwн were not sweet *for Jonah*; hence, Jonah delayed announcing them to Nineveh.

The words of Yнwн were especially bitter for Saul, from beginning to end. Yнwн gave instructions for Samuel to anoint Saul to a kingship that embodied the rejection of both Yнwн and Samuel himself (1 Sam. 8.7-9), so Saul did not stand a chance from the beginning of his reign. And at the end of Saul's days Samuel returned from the dead to drive the point home that Yнwн has become Saul's enemy (see 1 Sam. 28.15-19), and the narrator gave Saul a double death—he died the first time by falling on his own sword (1 Sam. 31.1-7), and he died a second time at the hand of an Amalekite (2 Sam. 1.1-10). Saul was rejected several times, and he was literarily killed twice. Yнwн's words to and about Saul were deadly. Whether the undisclosed proclamation of Yнwн was as toxic for Jonah cannot be determined, but the association of Jonah with Saul raises the possibility that Jonah was troubled by the proclamation that he was commanded to deliver to Nineveh.

My aim here is not to determine what Yнwн commanded Jonah to deliver, but to show how both the proclamation of Yнwн and the character of Jonah are problematic. I am not as interested in content, but on the impact of Yнwн's command upon the person and vulnerable body of Jonah (see Chapter 5). The proclamation of Yнwн was expected to be troublesome against Nineveh, but it could also have troubled Jonah, who was vulnerable but not submissive. In this frame, i hear the vulnerable Jonah moving away from the shadows of Yнwн when he announced, "Forty days more, and Nineveh shall be overthrown." In this reading, Jonah extended the deadline to forty days in order to give Nineveh, his people (according to the Qur'an in 10.98 and 37.147), a chance.

90 *Jonah*

Third, Jonah does not use the expected "thus says the LORD" messenger formula (see Ward 1991) but instead he "cried out" as if the proclamation was his own (Jon. 3.4). And in the ears of Nineveh, the proclamation was Jonah's. There is no reason, on the basis of the announcement itself, for Nineveh to associate Jonah's proclamation with God/YHWH. So why did Nineveh believe אלהים, fasted and put on sackcloth (Jon. 3.5)? One possible answer is that they trusted Jonah.

The above reflections problematize the popular assumption that Jonah was in support of YHWH against Nineveh. There are several reasons, even in a reading backward process, for Jonah to be on a different page from YHWH.

Believing in Nineveh

In light of the reflections discussed here, i propose that Jonah adjusted the proclamation that he was given. Nineveh's response to Jonah was (in narrative time) immediate: in the next verse, the narrator reports that Nineveh believed אלהים and began rituals of repentance (they fasted and grieved). In the case of Nineveh, there is no delay or separation in the account by the narrator. The narrative is swift, and so was Nineveh. I suggest two possible explanations for Nineveh's haste.

First, the quick response of Nineveh may have been because they felt sorry for Jonah. Nineveh saw a tired (having walked for a whole day) and vulnerable (as argued in Chapter 5) Jonah and they wanted him to rest. Nineveh was compassionate towards and sympathetic with Jonah, who on the basis of the Qur'an (as proposed in Chapter 5) came to Nineveh as part of his healing process. In this view, Nineveh showcased what it means to love one's enemies (insofar as the biblical version is concerned) as one's own (according to the Qur'anic version, Nineveh is not enemy territory). The people of the city believed אלהים and started rituals of repentance because they wanted Jonah to stop his diatribe. And, it worked. Jonah stopped his tirade and he did not walk to the end of the city (another two days away). Nineveh thus gave Jonah a rest, and the chance to recover and to heal.

Second, the quick response of Nineveh may have been out of fear, and so they were hoping that their אלהים will save them from the overthrow that Jonah announced. In this view, Nineveh did not take Jonah and אלהים to be on the same side. The אלהים that Nineveh believed does not even have to be the same as the YHWH whose proclamation troubled Jonah. I nonetheless imagine that the אלהים whom Nineveh believed (in Jon. 3.5) is the same as the אלהים (in Jon. 3.8-9) whom the king instructed Nineveh to appease. The king's explanation may thus be rendered, "Who knows, [our] אלהים may return and relent, and turn back his face, so that we do not perish" (Jon. 3.9). In this rendering, the king wants the אלהים of Nineveh (read: God of the city) to come back, to turn back his face to Nineveh, so that the city is saved from Jonah's overthrow. This reading assumes that Nineveh had their own native אלהים who had left them or had let them down, so the objective of the city was to make their אלהים "return" to them. They were afraid of Jonah, and they wanted their (national, native) אלהים to protect them.

6. A City That Believed

91

Both explanations favour Nineveh, echoing the favour that both אלהים (in Jon. 3.10) and Yʜwʜ (in Jon. 4.11) extended towards the city. Both אלהים and Yʜwʜ are present in Jon. 3.1-10 (Yʜwʜ in 3.1-3a, אלהים in 3.3b-10) and they are not confused or interchanged in the explanations offered here. In affirming Nineveh and their אלהים, the *return* to Jon. 3.1-10 made in this chapter appreciates Nineveh as a figure (or foil) for natives or people of the land. As an EBC reading of Jon. 3.1-10, this chapter thus lifts the "city" mask and burden (as in *fakatomala*) from Nineveh so that native faces and native אלהים are visible and engaged. It was that native אלהים that the city believed.

Chapter 7

A FISH THAT VOMITED (JON. 1.17–2.10)

Then the fish swallowed him, while he was blameworthy.
And had he not been of those who exalt Allah,
He would have remained inside its belly until the Day they are resurrected.

Qur'an (37.142-4, Sūrah Aṣ-Ṣaffāt; SAHIH International)

The passage cited from the Qur'an starts off with the fish but it quickly turns to Jonah, who is its main concern. Jonah was blameworthy, and that appears to be a sufficient reason to eliminate any question concerning why he was swallowed by the fish. The Qur'an is not bothered that the belly of the fish might not have been an appropriate place of segregation for Jonah's crime, but it gives the impression that he was guilty of something so very terrible that he was supposed to be in solitary confinement for a very long time (until the day of resurrection). Jonah's days have expired, and the fish was a "maximum prison" for him.[1]

While crime and punishment are at the background of the Qur'an passage, the key focus is on something that is seen as a positive characteristic, namely, that Jonah was among those who exalt Allah (see also Chapter 4). This characteristic saved him from being stuck in the belly of the fish until the day of resurrection (which could be during or beyond his lifetime). The Qur'an, however, does not state if Jonah exalted Allah while he was in the belly of the fish (as in the biblical narrative), and it is not clear if whatever he did while in the fish had any impact on the Qur'anic impression of him. Jonah could have been silent in the belly of the fish, and so his positive characteristic may be in reference to what he did before the fish swallowed him down. Notwithstanding the Quran's ambiguity, Jonah was released from confinement to the belly of the fish on account of a positive characteristic—he was among those who exalted Allah.

The unnamed fish, on the other hand, does not have any characteristics in the Qur'an. It did not have the capacity to hear and obey Allah, to notice that it had

---

1. Similar to the Hebrew Bible, the Qur'an prescribes rules, declares guilt and delivers punishment but it does not build or develop systems or structures for incarceration and correction. Both canons postulate and mete out punishment (ranging from fines and exclusion from the community all the way to capital and cooperate punishment) for mischievous characters, but neither has prison or penal facilities.

swallowed Jonah, to hear and feel what Jonah might have said or done while he was in its belly, or even to spew Jonah out. The fish was simply a vessel. It swallowed Jonah, but it did not vomit him out as in the biblical version. With regard to the biblical version, the belly of the fish as the context in which Jonah prayed does not impact how Jon. 2.1-10 is usually read. Put another way, this is a fish story in which the fish does not really matter. In response to this kind of leaning, i return in this chapter with a reading of Jon. 2.1-10 in which the fish, as vessel and context, matters. Two native assumptions flow through the following reading: first, the belly of the fish was like both a maximum prison (a place where many people find a lot of time for prayer) and a sanctuary (a place of security, as the bush was for Jonah) and second, the fish was affected by what Jonah said and did in its belly.

Fish matters

The double placements of one verse—"Yhwh provided a great fish to swallow Jonah; and Jonah remained in the gut of the fish for three days and three nights"— is the stimulus for the reading proposed in this chapter. This verse is at two places, Jon. 1.17 in the NRSV but Jon. 2.1 in the Hebrew Bible. What did the same verse signify at the end of Jonah 1 as compared to the beginning of Jonah 2?

In the NRSV, Jonah 1 ends with the reference that the fish swallowed Jonah. At this placement the verse gives the impression that the fish rescued Jonah from the sea[2] and detained him for three days and three nights.[3] It was going to be a short stay (compared to the intention to keep him until the day of resurrection in the Qur'anic passage), and the NRSV separates the fish swallowing Jonah from what Jonah does in Jonah 2. The opening verse of Jonah 2 in the NRSV shifts the focus to Jonah's prayer, and at the end of the prayer the chapter closes with a reference that the fish vomited Jonah out. The NRSV thus splits the fish story between Jonah 1 (where the fish swallowed Jonah) and Jonah 2 (where the fish vomited Jonah). And Jonah 2 in the NRSV is first of all about Jonah's prayer, with the fish presented as having vomited Jonah out in response to the prayer.

In the Hebrew Bible, on the other hand, the fish story is intact in the same chapter. Jonah 2 opens with the reference that the fish swallowed Jonah, and it closes with the reference that the fish vomited him out. The fish thus envelopes (read: swallows) Jonah's prayer; structurally, Jonah 2 in the Hebrew Bible presents Jonah's prayer as coming from the gut of the fish (Jon. 2.1). The fish swallowed Jonah in obedience to Yhwh, and vomited him out in response to Jonah's prayer.

While i stated in Chapter 1 that i follow the NRSV division of verses and chapters for practical reasons, the double placements of the verse in question make

---

2. In the eyes of the people of the sea, the rescue was not necessary because the sea had already calmed down.

3. Jonah's temporary detainment is presented as punishment for having fled from Yhwh and it has correctional intentions—to stop him from running (see also Sūrah 37.140-1).

94   *Jonah*

a difference for the reading of the fish and Jonah's prayer in this chapter. As the opening remark in the Hebrew Bible version of Jonah 2, this verse requires that Jonah's prayer be heard in the context of the fish. How might the fish have reacted to what it heard in Jonah's prayer? The fish may not have been able to speak to Jonah, but i expect that it would have heard and understood Jonah's words. The fish heard and obeyed YHWH's order for it to vomit Jonah out, so why not hear the prayer of Jonah as well? And, like the *b'hemah* of Nineveh that responded to the king's order to fast, repent and call on God, why couldn't the fish also respond appropriately to the words of Jonah? With my questions and assertions, i swim in the fantasy world of the narrative and imagine that the fish could hear Jonah.

Which context matters for the interpretation of biblical texts is a critical issue here. As i called attention in previous chapters to the sea (see Chapter 2), Nineveh (see Chapter 3), the hinterland (see Chapters 4 and 5) and the city (see Chapter 6), so i invite here seeing the fish as a context for reading Jonah's prayer. It is too easy, metaphorically speaking, to frame the fish for display among other novel catches and to discount the narrative as a work of fiction that drifts in the illusions of reality (the conclusion reached in most commentaries). Reality is not my main concern here; reality is fishy, anyways.

The reason and excuse for my interest in reading for the fish should be obvious— because i prefer to read for characters that are ignored and sidelined. And it makes a difference that i am a Pasifika native who loves and depends on what Tuvaluans call "home of the fish" (*fale o ika*), referring to the saltwater sea (bearing in mind that some fish make their home in freshwater as well). The following reading proposes possibilities of what Jonah's prayer might mean in the eyes and home of the fish. I first reflect on the place of the fish as the frame (Jon. 1.17–2.1, 10) for Jonah's prayer (focusing on the place of the fish among those who swallow and vomit), then i read Jonah's prayer backward in two parts: Jon. 2.7-9 (Jonah among those who pay up) and Jon. 2.2-6 (Jonah among those who are brought up).

Among those who swallow and vomit (Jon. 1.17–2.1 and Jon. 2.10)

The fish is in a special group of biblical characters that swallows (בלע, Jon. 1.17) objects. This group includes withered and thin ears of grain (Gen. 41.7), serpents (Exod. 7.12), earth (Exod. 15.12), the ground (Num. 16.30), YHWH (Ps. 21.9), the deep (Ps. 69.15), She'ol (Prov. 1.12), the wicked (Prov. 19.28) and fools (Eccl. 10.12). These biblical characters swallow objects in order to remove, punish or destroy them (see, for example, Job 8.18, 10.8). The fish in the Jonah narrative, on the other hand, did not destroy one of the objects that it swallowed. The doubly placed verse noted earlier (Jon. 1.17) quickly qualifies that Jonah is expected to be in the gut of the fish for only three days and three nights.[4] So the intention was not

---

4. Compare with the Qur'an version, in which Jonah was "sentenced" to be in the belly of the fish until the day of resurrection.

to destroy Jonah, but to briefly detain him. The fish was prepared by Yʜwʜ (Jon. 1.17), who later spoke to the fish to vomit Jonah out onto dry land (Jon. 2.10). And the text gives the impression that Jonah remained intact if not the same when the fish vomited him out again.

The fantasies of the narrative fail my islander experiences and imaginations. I imagine, on the other hand, that the usual wear and tear expected to take place in the belly of a fish would have withered the body of Jonah (similar to the bush), so the climax of this fish story is that the swallowed body of Jonah was not annihilated in the process. In the shadows of the bush and the city (which, against both proclamation and expectation, was not annihilated), and in light of the backward readings in the previous chapters, the story gives the impression that something in the fish repented and thus allowed Jonah to survive. In this connection, the fish for Jonah was like אלהים for the city of Nineveh. In addition to making for a better and islander fish story, this intersecting possibility situates the fish in a deeper (albeit *talanoa*) position among other biblical characters that swallow.

While many biblical characters swallow, only the land (Lev. 18.25, 28), the wicked (Job 20.15) and the fish (Jon. 2.10) also vomit.[5] The wicked will be made to vomit out the riches that he has stolen, whereas the land and the fish swallow and vomit human persons out. The association between the land and the fish is inviting with regard to both the fish (as swallower and one that vomited) and Jonah (as one who was both swallowed and vomited).

In Lev. 18.25, 28 and 20.22 the land (ארץ) vomits people out for the reason that those people have defiled the land. In these texts, defilement is understood in relation to the rules of God. The people who do not keep the rules of God defile the land, and they are therefore to be removed from the land. Two of the ways of removing such people are first, for the land to swallow them up and second, for the land to vomit them out. In both ways, the aim is to regain, reestablish and protect the sanctity of the land.

There are in the Hebrew Bible other ways to remove people who defile the land, such as being wiped out by the so-called mighty acts of God or by being carried away in the hands of foreign nations like Assyria and Babylon. What is significant with the texts that present the land as swallower and vomiter is that they accentuate the agency of the land. These biblical imageries make reasonable sense in cultures where the land is seen in human forms, for example, as mother(land),[6] consumer

---

5. Compare with Prov. 23.8 and 25.16, in which the subject that vomits is the one whom the sage addressed.

6. Related to the motherland image are the so-called sleeping lady mountain ranges like Kolobangara (Solomon Islands), Kosrae (Micronesia) and Huahine (Ma'ohi Nui). These are mountains that, from a distance, appear as the shape of a woman lying on her back with her head, breasts and stomach facing up (Kolobangara deserves a special mention here because it can be seen as a woman figure from two different sides of the island). The legends around these mountains are around fertility: the "sleeping lady" faces up (she is ignorantly turned over in Disney's *Moana* in which Te Fiti lies on her stomach) to receive rain, and gives birth

(with a mouth and guts), judge or thinker. The land as judge and thinker are connected in the Rotuman proverb, *the land has teeth and knows the truth* (*Pear ta Ma 'on Maf*, see Hereniko 2004). The land bites those who abuse or twist "the truth," which is understood to refer to any acts that insult or violate the *tapu* (taboo, sacredness) of the land. These acts may include shifting customary boundaries, disturbing burial grounds, uprooting sacred plants, shortcutting fishing and plantation rituals, making loud and unnecessary noises (especially on ceremonial sites), introducing nonnative practices and so on. Every (is)land has protocols that determine "the truth" of and for the land, and the land will bite the people (native and nonnative) who violate those rules and customs.

The philosophy of the Rotuman proverb is shared by natives from other Pasifika islands, to various decrees. Some islanders observe the cultural protocols tighter than others, both at the home island and in diaspora.[7] Like the rules of God with respect to the land of biblical Israel, so are the native protocols for the (is)lands of Pasifika. To stay long on the land, people need to keep "the truth" according to those rules and protocols. In other words, to borrow one of the critical challenges by Yothu Yindi, the land is not $40,000 or more but 40,000 years of tradition. In the eyes of indigenous Australians, the land is not "young and free" (a phrase in Australia's national anthem) but ancient and traditioned; the land is like an elder, a bearer of memory and wisdom. In this connection, the land may rightly swallow and/or vomit out occupants that violate its sanctity.

In associating the fish with the land, being two biblical subjects that both swallow and vomit, this reading brings the sea into the eyes of dry land. The upshot of this juxtaposition is that Jonah thereby becomes associated with people which the land swallowed or vomited out. That is, Jonah was among those who defile the land, which interconnects with the sea. In light of the Qur'an and the Pasifika insights noted above, the guilt of Jonah had something to do with violating the *tapu* of the land and sea. This reading highlights Jonah's failure to inquire and observe the protocols of the land of Nineveh, but instead he walked through and spoke as if he belonged (he does in the Qur'an but not in the biblical narrative) and would be welcomed (see Chapter 6).

At the end of Jonah 2, the fish vomited Jonah out and then dies a literary death. This claim also affirms native home-of-fish (*fale o ika*) knowledge that a fish dies after it vomits. A fish that vomits is a dead fish. The landing (delivery) of Jonah onto dry land therefore marks the death of the fish. As the fish envelopes or frames Jonah's prayer, the dead fish reading invites reconsideration of Jonah's prayer and how it may have made the fish vomit. There are other ways for the fish to excrete

to plants and new life. In native Pasifika, therefore, the motherland is about plant (rather than human) life.

7. Ironically, the islanders who live in diaspora tend to be more traditionalist compared to the islanders who continue to live in the home islands. Removed from their home*land* makes the islanders in diaspora hold on tighter to native cultures and traditions, especially when they are not completely at *home* in their new location.

7. A Fish That Vomited 97

the contents of its gut, but to vomit suggests that something had upset it. So what in Jonah's prayer might have upset the fish? My query here recalls and extends White's concluding words: *"The reader both identifies with and condemns Jonah, demanding a reassessment of the religious community's relationship with God that pertains equally to men and women"* (White 1992: 214; my italics), and proceeds in the following sections in the interests of the land and the fish.

Among those who pay up (Jon. 2.7-9)

Yнwн envelopes (or frames) the second part of Jonah's prayer. This part opens with Jonah remembering (זכר) Yнwн (Jon. 2.7) and closes with Jonah committing to sacrifice and pay up what he had vowed to Yнwн. Fulfilling these commitments is expected to bring "deliverance for Yнwн" (Jon. 2.9). In between the Yнwн-frames Jonah presents himself with confidence and hints of self-righteousness, in contrast to "the ones who heed lying breaths [and] forsake their own mercy" (Jon. 2.8). Jonah is better than those people because he will pay up; he will fulfil what he vowed. He is better off also because, suggested by the structure of the prayer, he is enveloped (or protected) by Yнwн.

Remix

Jonah remixed the "memory game" and turned it upon Yнwн, the biblical character who is better known for occasionally remembering commitments that he had made. Yнwн must have forgotten his commitments for some time, but that is not acknowledged. What matters is that Yнwн has remembered (regained memory), and he acted on what he had committed (covenanted). One of the examples of this is the regaining of Yнwн's memory that sparked the exodus:

> A long time after that, the king of Egypt died. The Israelites were groaning under the bondage and cried out; and their cry from the bondage rose up to God. God heard their moaning, and God remembered (זכר) His covenant with Abraham and Isaac and Jacob. God looked upon the Israelites, and God took notice (ידע) of them. (Exod. 2.23-4, NJPS)

Jonah remixed this exodus memory in his prayer by presenting himself as the subject of the verb זכר (remember, take notice) with Yнwн as the one that is remembered (Jon. 2.7). Yнwн remembered (זכר) and recognized (ידע) Israel in the exodus memory game, but Jonah remembered and prayed (a form of recognition) to Yнwн in Jon. 2.8.[8] Jonah did not "cry from the bondage" (as the Israelites did) but his prayer came into the holy temple. The regain of Jonah's memory led to his

---

8. The agency of Jonah as the *subject that remembered* is disguised in the NJPS translation: "When my life was ebbing away, I called the LORD to mind (זכר)" (Jon. 2.8a).

98 *Jonah*

prayer (in words) and he followed this up with his commitment (with words still) to pay up, with the intention that this will spark deliverance. In Jonah's case, the deliverance is for Yнwн (see Chapter 2). Whereas Yнwн remembered and worked to deliver Israel, here Jonah remembered and planned to deliver Yнwн. Jonah has thus taken over the place of Yнwн in the memory game. Yнwн is not the one who remembered and delivered, but Jonah.

Jonah's remix of the memory game invites rereading of other narratives relating to the regain of memory, around the questions of *who delivers* and *who is delivered.* Two narratives are relevant for this EBC study because they are related to land and women. First is the narrative of Sarai, the barren (Gen. 11.30) wife of Abram the wealthy slaveowner (Gen. 12.5) whose ancestral roots go back to Ur of Chaldea. The pain of Sarai's barrenness reached a critical point in Genesis 15, where Abram lamented that he does not have an offspring to inherit the occupied lands that the LORD showed him. Sarai took things into her own hands in Genesis 16 and pushed her Egyptian maidservant Hagar to be a concubine/wife for Abram so that she (Sarai) might have a son through her. This move worked, and Abram's firstborn was Ishmael.

After some time, Yнwн remembered and visited (פקד) the newly named Sarah and she bore Abraham's second son, Isaac (Gen. 21.1-8). The second son became heir to Abraham's inheritance because Sarah pushed Ishmael with his mother Hagar out of the household. The narrative continues with more twists and turns, but my focus here is on which character was delivered in this narrative. Five are obvious: Sarai was delivered from barrenness, Abraham was delivered from not having an heir, Yнwн was delivered from not fulfilling the promise of an offspring for Abraham, Israel was delivered from having to account for Abraham's firstborn and patriarchy was delivered with its procreation agenda. The connection between the regaining of memory and deliverance is rich and complex in this narrative.

Second is the narrative of Bethlehem (בת-לחם) the "house of bread" (in Tongan, this is a *feleoko*, which is the dryland version of the Tuvaluan *fale o ika*) that suffered a famine during the time of the judges (Ruth 1.1). The famine of Bethlehem (compare with the barrenness of Sarai) pushed the family of Elimelech, Naomi, Mahlon and Chilion to seek refuge in the land of Moab.[9] Elimelech died at Moab and Naomi married off their two sons to two Moabite women, Ruth (for Mahlon)

---

9. In the narrative world, there are several gaps that beg for further details: other families from Bethlehem probably set out as refugees, and to other lands, but the narrative privileges the family of Elimelech and Naomi. I imagine that this narratively privileged family, similar to the family of Abram and Sarai, had wealth, resources and helpers that enabled them to flee and find asylum during a stressful time. I imagine also that the family of Elimelech and Naomi, like the family of Rahab (Joshua 2), had neighbours who could not afford to flee but who survived the famine. Their neighbours would not have shared the narrator's appreciation for the return of Naomi, who seems to have returned and set up home in the family property that they had abandoned. Unless Naomi brought Ruth to stay with the redeemer of Elimelech's inheritance, this has implications for the unfolding of the

and Orpah (for Chilion). The two sons also died, leaving Naomi with two widowed daughters-in-law. When Naomi heard that YHWH had remembered and visited (פקד) his people, which is a way of saying that the famine has ended and the people have food (לחם), she started out to return to Bethlehem with both daughters-in-law (Ruth 1.6-7). On the way, Naomi told her daughters-in-law to return each to her mother's house (Ruth 1.8). Against Naomi's direction, both widows insisted on going with her to her people (Ruth 1.9-10). At Naomi's second bidding (Ruth 1.11-13), Orpah returned home (from somewhere on the road, outside of town) but Ruth went on towards the land and the inheritance of her late husband and father-in-law. The story continues, but i return to my question—who in this narrative are delivered due to the regain of YHWH's memory? The land of Bethlehem (בת-לחם) was delivered from uncharacteristically not having food (לחם, bread) for its people, YHWH was delivered from forgetting Bethlehem and its people, Naomi was delivered from having to live as a widow in a foreign land and Orpah was delivered from the eyes of ruthless readers. In this narrative, too, the connection between regain of memory and deliverance is rich and complex.

In the narratives of Sarai and Bethlehem, YHWH is among those who are delivered. In this regard, Jonah's remix is not on its own, as if its foreign or strange, in biblical memory. But his remix could have irritated the fish, which became upset upon hearing that Jonah was seeking deliverance for YHWH. I suggest this reading in light of Jon. 1.17, in the context of which the deliverance of YHWH meant that YHWH will not be held accountable for forcing the fish to swallow something that was foreign to its world. Put more directly: hearing that YHWH is to be delivered was bad enough to make the fish upset and vomit, and then died.

Closet

I suggested above that Jonah was confident and somewhat self-righteous in Jon. 2.8 because YHWH enveloped or framed him, which is to say that YHWH protected and sheltered him. The same protection could also be confining, similar to the way that a fence protects, limits as well as prohibits. Such effects are present in the imagery of the closet in the lives of LGBTQI people. In this regard, the gut of the fish was Jonah's proverbial closet. Michael Carden reached a similar conclusion in his queer commentary:

> I believe Jonah's flight from and subsequent acceptance of his mission can be read as an allegory of coming out. Jonah opens with the prophet challenged to take a message of judgement to Nineveh. Instead he flees to the other end of the world, taking ship to Tarshish. While on board he hides himself in the hold. When thrown overboard, he is swallowed by a fish and is engulfed in "the deep" (2.6). . . . This language of flight in quest of an illusory security strongly evokes

narrative. I develop these sorts of hidden (untold, un-remembered) details in my forthcoming commentary on Ruth.

the experience of the closet. The mention of the temple serves to remind me that for many people the closet is embraced on religious grounds. (Carden 2006: 466–7)

By extension, the temple towards which Jonah prayed was a religious and cultural closet. Without lessening the pain in the coming-out experience, non-LGBTQI people too feel constrained by the protection that they receive from others (who put them in closets) including God.

The cultures of reciprocity in Pasifika, where both LGBTQI and non-LGBTQI people function and prosper, are confining because they require one "to do likewise" unto others. Whether one agrees regarding what to do, values the reciprocal practice, is not important. Rather, what one receives from one's family and extended relations determines how one is to live and reciprocate. In this regard, the protection that one receives, no matter if they appreciate it, is a burden to do likewise. Reciprocity, with all its advantages for Pasifika natives, is burdensome in this regard especially for people who do not have the means and resources to reciprocate.

The cultures of covenant-keeping in the Bible are confining in a similar way. A later generation is obliged to observe agreements made three and four generations earlier, whether the later generation understands or accepts (in the same way) the covenantal terms or not. The benefits of covenant-keeping are not questioned here, for they help keep order and peace in the covenant community. Covenants are nonetheless confining upon covenant-makers, including God. God is obliged and confined to the covenant (when he remembers), which is taken here to be another proverbial closet.

As reciprocity and covenant cultures envelope and frame generations, so are the whiffs of confidence and self-righteousness that come out in Jon. 2.8. Did Jonah realize that he was in several closets? On account of this question, i wonder if the fish vomited when it realized that it, like the temple, was a proverbial closet for Jonah. As many people do not appreciate being seen as bullies and tyrants (read: closets), even though they obviously are, so do i imagine in the case of the fish. The fish was upset and it vomited when it realized that it was a sanctuary that was also a closet.

Among those who are brought up (Jon. 2.2-6)

Continuing to read backward, the first half of the prayer opens with Jonah's call coming from out of his troubles and ends with his confidence that YHWH raised (read also in the future sense: will raise) him out of the deep. Place is ambiguated in the prayer, which locates Jonah at Sheol, the sea, the deep and the pit, but does not mention the fish (the obvious location in Jon. 1.17). The prayer is poetic, sucking readers into its rhythm and rip. Time and grammar ebb and flow in this prayer, upon the currents of poetry and orality, but the assertion is clear: that

7. A Fish That Vomited   101

Jonah cried out, and Yhwh responded and delivered him. How might this upset the fish?

The sea is the home for and of fish (*fale o ika*), so fish in (sea)water are the equivalent of "people of the land" in the mind of humans (*qua* land creatures). The fish was among the native creatures of the sea. There are other living creatures in the sea including plants and corals, but the narrative focuses on one, a great (גדל) fish,[10] which is a way of saying that this fish was one of the "elders" of the sea. The fish was great not just because of its size but also because of its status in the sea. This was a noble fish, a great elder in the sea, and attention to and concerns about its lot invites reconsideration of the lot of other native elders on dry land as well. For guidance (and because i am not a fish) i turn back to the two narratives i discussed above.

The lands to be inherited in the narratives of Sarai were not *terra nullius*. They were already occupied by native people of the land:

> On that day the LORD made a covenant with Abram, saying, "To your descendants I assign this land, from the river of Egypt to the great river, the river Euphrates, *the land of* the Kenites, the Kenizzites, the Kadmonites, the Hittites, the Perizzites, the Rephaim, the Amorites, the Canaanites, the Girgashites, and the Jebusites." (Gen. 15.18-21, NRSV; my italics)[11]

The people of the land are named, and they are to be pushed away together with Hagar and Ishmael. The native people of the land are like "great fish" on dry land, to be vomited out in order to privilege the memory of Abraham, Isaac and Jacob.

Bethlehem was one of the lands that was grabbed due to the covenant that Yhwh made with Abram, and the name continues today in a Palestinian town in the West Bank. It was out of Bethlehem that Micah expected a ruler for Israel to come:

> And you, O Bethlehem of Ephrath,
> Least among the clans of Judah,
> From you one shall come forth
> To rule Israel for Me—
> One whose origin is from of old,
> From ancient times. (Micah 5.1, NJPS)

The last two lines are inviting because the "one whose origin is from old, from ancient times" could be applied to three characters—Yhwh, Israel, or the land of

---

10. Compare to the Qur'an version, which does not identify the fish as "great." Whether this is supposed to mean that this was a regular fish or that there were other fish in the sea that could swallow people, the text is teasing.

11. Compare with the NJPS translation, which names the people but ambiguates how they are connected to the land that has been promised to the descendants of Abram.

Bethlehem from which the ruler will come. Since the verses that follow disclose Micah's expectations concerning this ruler, i take Bethlehem as the "one whose origin is from old, from ancient times." Bethlehem was ancient before Micah expressed his desire, and even before Rachel gave birth to Ben-Oni (but his father called him Benjamin) then died and was buried near there (Gen. 35.19). Micah thus opens up a window for identifying the ruler to come with the ancient Bethlehem—before the time when Naomi returned and found that people of Bethlehem survived the famine and absence of Yhwh, and before the interests of Israel overtook the biblical world. Bethlehem had people of the land in the ancient times before biblical Israel occupied it, and their descendants have struggled with occupation and displacement up to the segregation walls of the modern state of Israel.

The narrative of Bethlehem in the book of Ruth refers to another ancient land, Moab, where Naomi found refuge for some time. In the eyes of biblical Israel, Moab is among the godforsaken lands (cf. Gen. 19.30-8). But as the narrative unfolds in the book of Ruth, it was through the body of a Moabite widow, Ruth and her second husband from Bethlehem, Boaz, that a ruler for Israel was raised. In this connection, Micah's ruler came forth out of Bethlehem and his roots go back to ancient Moab.[12]

In the eyes of the people of the land, the narratives of Sarai and Bethlehem are narratives of displacement. But the displaced are not erased; they are present even in the houses of the rulers of biblical Israel. How might the big fish, as an elder of the sea, react to the treatment of these elders of the land? In this reading, the great fish serves as a reminder of natives of land and sea that are sunk into the pits of memory. I imagine the fish wishing that they are not forever forgotten and, borrowing the words of Maya Angelou, that *still they rise*!

Dead fish

I raised questions that cannot be answered with confidence or righteousness, and proposed readings of Jonah's prayer that are fishy (pun intended). The fish was not human so it would not have pondered over my questions and readings, but this EBC work dives into the world of the narrative and upsets the tendency to think of the fish (and other creatures of the sea) as mindless, unimportant and dispensable. This fish might have been huge (גדול) in size and gut but with a small brain, yet it was a living and moving character in the narrative. While the Jonah narrative has many of the marks of fantasy and novelty, those do not give readers the licence to

---

12. Ruth is identified as a Moabite or foreigner for most of the book of Ruth. While this way of identifying her suggests racial discrimination (as a Moabite, Ruth is outsider par excellence), it also calls readers' attention to the place of Moab in the lineage of David. This is especially critical in cultures that follow matrilineal descent (e.g. a person with a Jewish mother is Jewish).

ignore the displacement of great natives (on dry land and in the sea) in ancient times or in biblical literature.

It matters in this EBC study that the fish swallowed and vomited, and i proposed (read: imagined, romanticized) possible explanations for what might have caused the fish to vomit because this signifies death for this great native of the sea. Whereas the land vomited in order that it may regain its *tapu* and continue to live, the fish vomited in Jonah 2 and then dies a literary death. In the readings proposed here, the fish died not (only or simply) because it was blameworthy but because it was upset with Jonah's prayer.

I have suggested possible explanations for why the fish vomited and died in part because the biblical narrator does not respect "the truth" of the sea (*fale o ika*), and in part out of respect for the fish as an unnamed and easily forgotten biblical character. Unlike the withered bush for which the vulnerable Jonah was prepared to die, the fish vomited then died a literary death away from the eyes of the narrator and readers. This EBC study, taking advantage of the fantasy world of this biblical narrative, invites understanding of and solidarity with a noble creature of the sea. On this note, and in closing, i return to the Qur'an, which spares the fish of the experience and implications of vomiting. According to Sūrah 37.145, Allah threw Jonah on land and so the fish did not have to vomit and die.

Deliverance for the fish!

Chapter 8

A BOAT THAT THOUGHT (JON. 1.4-16)

And indeed, Jonah was among the messengers.
[Mention] when he ran away to the laden ship.
And he drew lots and was among the losers.
Then the fish swallowed him, while he was blameworthy.

Qur'an (37.139-42, Sūrah Aṣ-Ṣaffāt; SAHIH International)

The Qur'an is selective with the details to include in its (re)telling (*talanoa*), and the gaps in its account tease the imagination of readers.[1] Narrative gaps are thresholds that draw readers into the worlds of the text as well as into the realms of narrative fantasy. With regard to the latter, in the Qur'an Jonah looks like an Arabian genie who is meant to be trapped in the belly of the fish (as a sea version of the desert lamp) because he did not have a master (who would rub the belly of the fish and release Jonah to perform miracles at his bidding). And the fish comes across as having the capacity, as in modern movies, to inhale or knock Jonah off from the deck (with such precision that he fell straight into its open mouth).[2] Along with the narrative gaps are details added in the Qur'an such as the reference to other losers, some of whom may have been on board the same laden boat and who may have been swallowed by the same fish. The gaps and excesses in the Qur'an version are opportunities for alternative readings.

Two characteristics of Jonah matter in the Qur'an and both appear to have been formed before the events at sea: when Jonah ran away to the loaded boat, he was a

---

1. These are gaps in relation to the biblical account, so this stage of *reading backward* continues to take advantage of the *reading forward* presented in Chapters 2 and 3. I prefer to speak of gaps rather than "hidden" or "omitted" dialogues (cf. Person Jr. 1996: 15–30) because i am upfront about my role in filling the gaps.

2. The biblical account avoids this complication because Jonah went down into the hold of the vessel and slept there when the storm hit, and the men threw him into the sea. These details give the narrative a shot of reality, and stop the *flight* of readers' mind.

8. A Boat That Thought

messenger as well as one who exalted Allah.[3] Because of these qualities,[4] Allah (pulled him out from the belly of the fish and) threw him onto the open shore. While on the boat, Jonah did one thing: he drew lots. He lost, and was swallowed by the fish. Whether he fell or was thrown (and by whom) from the boat[5] into the mouth of the fish, the Qur'an does not divulge. Because Jonah was taken to be blameworthy, it is easy to understand why there was no need to explain why he lost the draw. He must have been guilty of something great and unacceptable (but not necessarily because he ran away *from* someone or something[6]), so it was not necessary to explain or justify why he lost. But he was not the only loser. He was among other losers but they are not persons of interest in the Qur'an. Jonah is the main character, and the focus is on his lots.

The boat has one characteristic in the Qur'an: it was laden. Burdened. The boat was a vessel for transportation, like the fish, and a shelter, like the bush at the hinterland and the temple in Jonah's prayer (similar to the genie's lamp in Chinese and Arabian mythologies). Did these expectations contribute to the burdens of the boat? As i pondered with respect to the fish in Chapter 7, i wonder how the boat might have thought of what happened in the biblical account. I raise this possibility on account of Jon. 1.4b, which also translates as "the boat thought (חשב, in Piel Perfect form) about breaking up." The biblical narrative, with flares of novelty and remixing of reality, presents the boat as a vessel-and-shelter that could think, without denying that it was a human construction (like the city). In the following sections, building upon my reading of the city as an earthed character, i revisit Jon. 1.4-16 upon the textual premise that the boat was a "thinker" (rather than a "sleeper"—like Jonah in the boat—or a "sinker"—as the sailors feared). What did the boat think about what happened in and around it, as told (*talanoa*) in the biblical narrative?

Among those that think

The capacity to think is not a privilege of humans alone. Other living creatures have minds of their own (as most people who have one or more pets know), and some can also think in human terms as well as communicate with humans.

---

3. He was a messenger but, as far as the Qur'an is concerned, this does not mean that he had a message (of words) when he boarded the boat. As suggested in earlier chapters, i also take Jonah's body to be part of his message.

4. Jonah is also remembered as Dhul-Nūn (ذُو ٱلنُّون, "The One of the Fish," in Sūrah 68.46) and as an apostle of Allah (Sūrah 4.163 and 6.86). According to Islamic oral tradition, the prophet Mohammed spoke favourably of Jonah as a prophet like he.

5. I use "boat" for אניה because "ship" connotes a Western vessel among Pasifika islanders, and also because one of the subjects that oblige the reading offered in this chapter is commonly referred to as "boat people" (the refugees). See further explanation below.

6. The emphasis of Sūrah 37.140 is that Jonah ran away *to* the laden boat, rather than that he ran away *from* someone or something.

Animals and natives

The serpent in the Yahwist's garden story (Gen. 2.4b–3.24) is first among the Bible's wise characters that could speak and think. It spoke human language, it reflected on what it saw and heard, it understood what happened around it, it knew some of the truths about what was (not) good and (un)pleasant, it exposed that YHWH misled Eve and 'Adam about one tree in particular (they will not die if they eat from it as YHWH intimated), and it engaged Eve in a meaningful and captivating way. The serpent was wise, and Eve too was wise because she knew how to think and communicate in serpent terms and she decided on what she saw to be beneficial for her and her partner. In their exchange, both the serpent and Eve were wise characters. The serpent had something to teach Eve and 'Adam in the garden, and it continues to teach readers beyond the shadows of the tree of life (see Yee 2003: 59-79). And humans continue to live out Eve's decision, preferring knowledge and enlightenment[7] over blind adherence, but some wise humans have blamed Eve for the theological construction known as the "fall of humanity."

Balaam's ass is another character that could think in human terms (Numbers 22-4). It saw what Balaam could not see, it knew where to go and when to stop, it spoke and it followed directions. It too was a wise character, but many readers are quick to make light of its gifts. Who would think that something good or wise would come out of an ass's mouth? This question appeals to "ass" as reference to both an animal and a body part, and the animal loses out because a human ass is not considered among the "seats of wisdom." It might be for this reason that the ass is presented as feminine in Num. 22.28, given the androcentricity of the biblical world. But like Eve's serpent, Balaam's ass understood what happened around it and i consider her among those who are wise.

I take access to language and ability to communicate as indications that a character can think because language is necessary for constructing and disseminating wisdom. Access to language is needed in order for any character to think; and on the reverse side, no character can think without a language. So, in biblical narratives, the serpent and the ass could think because they could also speak, and i stretch the narrator's assessment of the serpent (that it was a shrewd character) to the ass—she too must have been shrewd.

I must confess that my interest in linking language with intelligence and wisdom is influenced by the *talanoa* cultures of Pasifika (see Chapter 3)—*talanoa* requires and at the same time constructs language—and in recognition of the ability of Pasifika islanders to be bilingual (without counting any of the European languages) at the very least. There are, for example, more than eight hundred living languages on the island of Papua (divided between PNG and West Papua), over one hundred languages in Vanuatu and over sixty languages in the Solomon Islands, and natives of these island groups grow up learning to communicate in at

---

7. Which have their own consequences, as in the climate effects of the industrial revolutions and the toxic output of the carbon civilization.

least two of their native languages.[8] In this connection, the multilingual Pasifika natives too are wise.

Natives and artificial intelligence

Biblical animals and Pasifika natives have access to language and can think, but could a boat possess those characteristics? I offer affirmative responses from two seemingly opposite cultural contexts.

First, from native Pasifika communities that project the pride that "our ancestors were navigators" in what we do and how we think, an affirmative response may be given to the question because the boats of our ancestors could think then in ancient times and continue to speak to and visit modern generations. An example of this is the phenomenon that we in Tonga call *vaka loa*, which several Pasifika islands share. This is when someone is about to die and the long (*loa*) boat (*vaka*)—the two words that make up *vaka loa*—of the ancestors comes to receive their soul and transport it to the home of the ancestors (which has many names, for example, *Pulotu, Sondo, Hawaiki*). The arrival of the *vaka loa* is announced the night before by the *fata* (a seabird that comes on land for special occasions)[9] calling from the home of the one who is about to depart. The *vaka loa* hears the voice of the *fata* and comes ashore when the dying one is ready to depart. In the evening after the departed soul has boarded the boat of the ancestors, the *fata* calls from the sea and the *vaka loa* knows how to re-enter the sea and return to the home of the ancestors. The landing and leaving of the *vaka loa* are heard in the waves making the distinct sound of a boat pulled on coral and sand. The *vaka loa* is thus not visible to native eyes, but it could be heard in the calling of the *fata* and in the murmurs of the waves. The *vaka loa* navigates itself between the realms of the ancestors, the living and the dying, and between the sea, the land and the underworld. In these regards, the *vaka loa* of the ancestors is among the wise characters in Pasifika mythologies and modern ears.

Second, in the dawning age of artificial intelligence (AI), in which robots and ships (in the air, the sea and on land) can think and respond (albeit according to the grids and matrices with which they have been coded) to what happen around them, a positive response to my question is reasonable. The AI bodies may not feel pain or fall sick (in human terms), but they can recode and develop their capacities and drives. As the cells of human bodies split, duplicate and multiply, so do the codes of the AI bodies. The AI bodies adapt and they are effective because their

8. Each of these three Melanesian groups has its own version of creole, which enables natives to communicate across indigenous language lines. While this common language assists with communication, "pidgin English" is nonetheless a colonial language—it is "broken English" but it functions with an "English" frame of mind.

9. The same bird has a different name when it is in the sea (*kiu*) and when it is on land (*fata*). When the *fata* calls out in the morning it announces conception (arrival); but when it calls out in the evening it announces death (departure).

108   *Jonah*

minds contextualize. Some AI bodies are in human forms (humanoids) and they take good care of elderly and sickly humans, as well as reinvent and update themselves (beyond the options available according to their codes). In the age of AI as well, my question is a no-brainer—boats can think!

The boat saw the fish

In the company of biblical animals that talk, of poly-lingual Pasifika natives, of Pasifika ancestral rites and of the technological advances of the AI generation, the biblical portrayal of the boat as a character that thinks is not totally strange. In such wise and illustrious company, a boat that thinks in Jon. 1.4 is simply fantastic (read also: laden with fantasies). How might the boat have seen in, and how might it have thought of, what took place in and around it in Jon. 1.4-16?[10]

A lot happened around and in the boat. Yhwh threw wind around, the sea stormed and people on deck were worried. The mariners threw baggage overboard, with the hope that this would benefit them first rather than the boat itself. The mariners rowed harder but could not reach shore, then they threw a man overboard. The boat would have seen all of those, as well as how the sea calmed down in response. It would have also seen how, for some reason, the men on board became afraid of Yhwh. They unexpectedly sacrificed a sacrifice and vowed vows to Yhwh, but uncharacteristically they did not check to see what happened to the man overboard. No one saw what happened to that man except for the boat, which was drifting in and popping above water. It would have seen the great fish swallow Jonah and thought of several explanations, such as two that come through the *talanoa* offered earlier: the boat could have seen the fish as if it was the *vaka loa* that has come to take Jonah to the ancestors, or it could have seen the fish as an AI ship that has come to abduct Jonah to the world of fantasies. Whatever the boat thought of what happened, i imagine that it would have been different from what the humans thought. The boat would not have any excuse to fear Yhwh, but good reasons to marvel at what the fish did. In this reading, the fish was an extension of the boat. I expect them to look out for one another, given that both are wise characters in the sea.

The fish vomited, but the boat was gagged. The narrative presented the boat as one that could think, but the narrative did not allow the boat to also have a voice. That task, i suggest, is for readers to follow through (cf. Chen 2004: 293).

Among those who are laden

In the Qur'an version, the boat was laden. This should not be an issue because a boat is meant to carry passengers and cargo so it is expected to be laden, and the

---

10. This question does not apply to the Qur'an version, where there is no storm and no stress on board.

load of a laden boat helps keep it steady in the water. In this regard, the boat would have appreciated Jonah going down into its belly (or "hold") to sleep (Jon. 1.5), for he lay down close to the boat's centre of gravity (known as "point G") below the waterline. And if there were other travellers sleeping there, all the better for steadying ("holding") the boat.

An empty or lighter boat is easier to toss around on the waves. As such, the boat would have felt the emptying out of its cargo, first the tossed baggage (Jon. 1.5) then a human body (Jon. 1.15) followed by victims that were sacrificed (Jon. 1.16), as making it lighter and more vulnerable. The mariners' response to the storm—they threw the baggage overboard to lighten things up for them (Jon. 1.5)—would not have been a wise move in the mind of the boat. The tossing of baggage was also unwise because those items become rubbish in the sea.

Laden seas

Everything thrown into the sea go somewhere—they sink to the seafloor, break up in the seawater, eaten by birds and sea creatures, or they are carried somewhere by the waves. All of these repercussions have devastating ecological impacts, especially with the plastic rubbish of the modern world that ends up in the sea. Plastic—one of the cheaper products of the Industrial Revolution—poisons marine lives, chokes and kills birds and sea creatures, and the rubbish that the waves carry away form into "floating islands" at several places in the Pacific Ocean between Indonesia and Hawaii. The mariners' solution—throw baggage (read: rubbish) into the sea—is devastating life systems in modern times. One of the upshots is that the sea is no longer wild. Rubbish reaches places that explorers fail to claim. But boats can see those impacts and devastations.

What the boat would have seen in relation to the mariners' solution is that it was not the only laden character in the narrative. The sea too was laden, both from the people's rubbish (baggage) and from Yhwh's wind. The narrative fixes the attention of readers to the storm on the surface of the sea, but the boat would have seen the effect of the storm under the waves. Storms disturb the seafloor and destroy the lifelines for and homes of sea creatures (*fale o ika*), and it takes many, many years for marine lives to recover from the devastation of one day's storm. Yhwh's wind may not have been as destructive as the raping of the seafloor that modern seabed mining operations do, but it would still take many years for the sea to recover. Both the quick devastation and the slow recovery would be visible to the boat, and would be cause for concern to a boat that could think.

Seabed mining operations involve AI bodies that could see deep beneath the seafloor. These operations take the "blue economy," which in Pasifika began circulation as reference to the harvesting and canning of fish (especially tuna) for profit, to another level. Seabed mining shares the goals of offshore oil and gas extraction (projects of the carbon civilization), to dig up and mine the resources and wealth under the seafloor for profit. Seabed mining operations are setting up at different islands around our deep "blue ocean," and in native minds they will also disturb the homes of our ancestors. While AI ships could see the riches under the seafloor and convert those into capital, they cannot feel the havoc they bring to the *fale o ika* nor the trouble that they cause for our ancestors. I imagine, on the other hand, that the boat in the biblical narrative could see and feel how the sea was laden. Unfortunately, this boat was gagged.

Boat people

Shifting into another platform (or deck), i also read the laden boat in the Qur'an as a pointer to laden boats outside of the canon including laden boats in the modern world that carry refugees. Such refugees are called "boat people" in Australia, and many of them are taken to be "processed" at detention centres located on Pacific Islands (Nauru, Manus) hence the detention and processing programme is known as the "Pacific solution." Many boats laden with boat people cross different seas in the world, and they see despair as well as hope, fear as well as courage, anxiety as well as comfort and so forth. In this regard, the boat in the biblical narrative would have seen more than what the narrator presented. It would have seen courage and hope in Jonah's solution—"Pick me up and cast me into the sea, and the sea shall calm against you"—as well as the rubbish in the mariners' solution. And assuming that this was not its maiden voyage, the boat would have seen different kinds of refugees come onto its deck.

International law assigns refugees into different categories, but it does not recognize climate refugees as legal. In Pasifika, notwithstanding, climate refuges were on the boats of our ancestors as well as on the boats that resettled communities from Banaba (Kiribati) to Rabi (Fiji) between 1945 and 1983, from Vaitupu (Tuvalu) to Kioa (Fiji) between 1947 and 1983, and from Phoenix (Kiribati) to Gizo (Solomon Islands) between 1954 and 1964. These forced migrants are not refugees in the eyes of international law, but they are received in Pasifika *because they were refugees.* They were forced to move, and they did not become stateless. In reality, the resettled people of Kioa are both Tuvaluan and Fijian, the resettled people of Rabi are both iKiribati and Fijian, and the Phoenix islanders are Solomon Islanders that have not given up being iKiribati as well. In Pasifika, climate refugees become bi-nationals.[11]

In Pasifika, climate refugees have joined the procession both across the seas and internally, including the 2005 resettlement of Carteret islanders (Papua New Guinea) and the 2014 resettlement of the Vunidogoloa village (Fiji). Given the acceleration of global warming, environmental scientists project that more communities from Tuvalu and Kiribati will be forced to move and resettle by 2050. Many homes in those communities are already flooded by the rising sea level, made worse once a month by the king tide that raises the water for four days or more at a time (see Figure 8.1).

---

11. Forced migration makes them bi-national and bi-cultural, but this reality has its side effects. For example, the second and third generations do not always feel that they belong back on their (grand)parents' home island and sometimes they feel out of place in their own homes.

Figure 8.1 A home flooded by rising sea level at South Tarawa, Kiribati. Photo: Siera Taniera and Cliff Bird, 2019.

What might the boat in the biblical narrative see in the lots of climate refugees?[12] After "the sea stood from its raging" (Jon 1.15), the crew and the passengers would have felt like they themselves were "boat people" and the boat would have endured a few knocks and nicks. If the boat with its passengers and cargo were to materialize in the modern age of AI and climate injustice, i imagine that they would consider voyaging in solidarity with climate refugees and protesting against seabed mining. I imagine also that they could be joined by the fleet of Pasifika *vaka loa* not to take away but to return the souls of the troubled and heavy laden in the modern world, as well as the troubled and heavy laden in the fantasized worlds of the Qur'an and the Bible.

Among those who are abandoned

When the great fish swallowed Jonah (Jon. 1.17), the narrator abandoned the boat at sea. Did the boat survive the sacrifice by the mariners? Did it need repairs? Did it (need to) reach shore? Did it find a resting place at the Mediterranean ship

---

12. The question moves backward and forward, to climate refugees that may have boarded the boat as well as climate refugees in recent times. The question looks into the narrative world, as well as at the lived worlds of readers.

graveyard? These questions bring to mind a teaching that oral tradition attributes to the Buddha (peace be upon him): you need a raft to cross a river; when you reach the other side you don't need the raft anymore so break it up, make a fire and warm yourself up. This teaching is very practical, so that one is not laden with carrying the raft on dry land (like the Levites who carried the tabernacle through the wilderness), but it does not take into consideration the interest of the raft or the benefit for other travellers who might come later and need to cross the same river.

In the biblical account, the boat is literarily abandoned. It did not even reach shore, where it might be broken up to feed a warming or cooking fire. Whereas Noah's ark came to rest on some memorable mountain, the Tarshish-bound boat was left drifting in the sea of the narrative towards the abyss of memory loss. And whereas Israel carried the ark of the covenant through the wilderness and rebuilt the Jerusalem temple after the exile, the boat-from-Joppa was a vessel that has served its function and it was no longer needed. No ancestral fish came to rescue the boat, and no scholarly community bothers to imagine its conditions or afterlife. The narrative rescued one man, and the great fish swam away with the interests and concerns of readers. In this context, and in light of the discussions in previous sections, the abandoned boat functions as a reminder of refugees who are ignored or abandoned by scholarly and international communities. Such privileged communities, especially when they ignore or choose not to see the underside of their privileges (see De La Torre 2019a: 40–80), are critiqued by grassroot(ed) activists and artists including Emmanuel Garibay (see Figure 1.4).

Emmanuel Garibay's *Prusisyon* (procession) challenges viewers to face up to and engage with climate refugees, who come in a procession towards the viewer (see Figure 8.2). The electricity posts and power lines indicate that the procession is over what used to be dry land, as well as suggest that power and development are behind (causing, pushing, forcing) the flight of climate refugees. *Prusisyon* is about (on land, internal) forced migration, and a reminder that climate refugees are not victims of some "natural" event. Rather, climate refugees are victims of human civilization and its images of power and progress.

Water rises up to the chest of a man carrying a son; on their side, a dog floats on a tube and reminds viewers that the devastation of climate change is not limited to humans. Animals are among the climate refugees. The dog faces away from the man and son as if in protest against (societies that approve) men who save their sons but let their daughters, wives and mothers drown. The bodies in procession are fenced by two heads. In front of the refugees is a ghostly ash-coloured clean-shaven head whose mouth drowns under water next to a foot kicking up into the air, and behind them is an oversize bearded head. The face on the bigger head behind the refugees may be read as expressing three conjectures: first, the eyes are closed as if this head does not want to see (compare to the open but blank- and frozen-eyed head at the foreground); second, the eyes are not tightly closed but tearing up (on the lower eyelids) as if this head identifies with and is sorry for the climate refugees; and third, the eyes are tearing up out of shame. The big head has multiple shades and expresses several meanings. The face that does not want to see is paler compared to the browned face of the climate refugees, and the pale face

Figure 8.2 Emmanuel Garibay, *Prusisyon* (oil on canvas, 2009). Used with permission of the artist.

that tears up in solidarity and/or out of shame is also tight-lipped and lacks emotions.

There is no boat in Garibay's *Prusisyon* in part because this work is about procession on land, but the big head floats like a boat on water. And in light of the foregoing *talanoa*, this big pale head ignores and is at once laden with the "lots" of brown-skinned climate refugees. In this connection, Garibay's *Prusisyon* may be taken as a critique of international law and pale systems that ignore, or are tight-lipped to, climate refugees who process before their very own eyes.

There is no boat in Garibay's *Prusisyon* also because for him boats represent colonization (as in his works under the title, *The Arrival*). Boats brought the power team of colonialists and missionaries to Asia and Pasifika, and i cannot rule out the possibility that the abandoned boat in the biblical narrative may have been one of those colonial boats. I, however, cannot affirm it either. No matter what kind of boat it was, it was still not appropriate to abandon it at sea especially if it had been damaged. In maritime law, to abandon a boat that was in distress may be treated as a crime.

114　　　　　　　　　　　　　　　*Jonah*

One of the gifts that one finds in the "folds" (or holds) of this novel is the possibility that the body of this one boat embodied the saying, "There were many boats in the sea." This one boat represented many boats, and this one boat had many characteristics. It was not just a simple vessel, but a complex biblical character as well. It thus could also have been the Mediterranean version of *vaka loa*. It came to pick up, to deliver and then return to the home of the ancestors. In this alternative view, the boat was not abandoned. Rather, it vanished (like the pirate boats of the Caribbean) from the eyes of ignoring and controlling readers. Deliverance. For the boat.

A sanctuary in motion

A boat is more than a vessel. It is also a floating, wayfaring, meandering sanctuary in the sense that it is a place where creatures find security, protection and rest. Here, sanctuary is not about comfort and it is not for humans alone. Rather, sanctuary is for all creatures who are displaced, troubled or threatened. In this regard, i am on the same boat as Miguel A. De La Torre: "The concept of sanctuary pre-dates the biblical text. Within ancient culture, those who feared death due to blood-feud retaliation or sanctioned execution could temporarily seek sanctuary at the altar of their local deity" (De La Torre 2019b: 157). In this light, one could see that the boat in Jon. 1.4-16 was a sanctuary on account of at least three events.

First, the boat was a sanctuary because, while the sea was storming up, Jonah felt secure enough to fall asleep in the boat. In the midst of the mayhem on deck, Jonah descended into the belly (hold, side) of the boat and went to sleep (Jon. 1.5). In this reading Jonah did not avoid the need to help out on deck (see Chapter 2), but he sought refuge somewhere close to "point G," and i imagine that he was not the only sleeper among the baggage (recalling the case of Saul, who was surrounded by other sleepers in 1 Sam. 26.5). There must have been others there who also found a place of safety, a sanctuary, for tired and distressed travellers and refugees.

Second, the boat was a sanctuary in the sense that prayers were offered from (Jon. 1.5), as well as demanded in (Jon. 1.6), there. The mariners on deck called on their אלהים (Jon. 1.5), Jonah was ordered to call (from the belly of the boat) on his אלהים (Jon. 1.6), and "the men" (also on deck) also cried to Yʜwʜ (Jon. 1.14). The boat was a sanctuary for naming and calling upon several Gods (so Vaka'uta 2014) and as such, to borrow the words of Bryan Cones and Stephen Burns, it was the kind of place that "points a way beyond talk of inclusion towards a generous embrace of the many differences that make up . . . community" (Cones & Burns 2019: xiv). Such a community exists on boats among boat people, and i imagine the same in the case of the boat in Jon. 1.4-16.

Third, vows and a sacrifice were offered, at the end, somewhere on the boat (Jon. 1.16). These rituals were not necessarily expressions of belief or conversion, but of recognition and gratitude for the deliverance that they have experienced. These rituals affirm that worship involves more than words, and that sanctuary is a place where, to appropriate the words of De La Torre, "acts that demonstrate solidarity with the oppressed" are embodied (De La Torre 2019b: 157). In this connection, the boat in Jon. 1.4-16 was a place where rituals of *solidary between oppressed people*—between the fearful mariners and travellers with Jonah the man overboard—were practiced.

In this reading, the boat in Jon. 1.4-16 was more than a troubled and abandoned vessel. It was also a sanctuary that moved on the face of the water and thus challenges the common expectation that a sanctuary needs to be stable and fixed. This boat was a sanctuary that was in motion, as was the fish and Jonah.

Chapter 9

A FLIGHT THAT CONTINUES (JON. 1.1-3)

And indeed, Jonah was among the messengers.
[Mention] when he ran away to the laden ship.

Qur'an (37.139-40, Sūrah Aṣ-Ṣaffāt; SAHIH International)

The Qur'an does not name from whom or what Jonah ran away, nor does it explain why. He was among "the messengers" (which means that he was a "prophet," to use a biblical title) when he ran away to the laden boat, and he is the one runaway messenger that reached the hallowed grounds of biblical literature. He fled from the presence of Yhwh, but he could not escape the strokes and traps of scripture.

In the Qur'anic version, Jonah ran away to a boat, a floating sanctuary that one expects to be in motion; in the biblical version, he ran away to a stationary but distant destination—Tarshish. The Qur'an orients Jonah's flight towards the sea; in addition, the Bible also orients Jonah's flight towards dry land—Tarshish—on the other side of the sea (compared to the *flow into the sea* orientation proposed in Chapter 2). Tarshish is not reached in both the Qur'anic and the biblical narratives, and it remains a riddle for readers. Why Tarshish? Does anything good come out of Tarshish? Where, or to whose presence, did the wickedness of Tarshish come up?[1] An inner-textual conversation takes place in this pericope: Yhwh saw Nineveh as wicked (Jon. 1.2) but Jonah drew attention to Tarshish (Jon. 1.3) as if to suggest that Tarshish too was wicked.

In this closing chapter i return to the opening passage in the Jonah narrative (Jon. 1.1-3), which also serves as the final stop in this *reading backward* exercise, and from that to the burdens of biblical commentary. With respect to Jon. 1.1-3, i focus my reflection on one detail in the biblical account which is not in the Qur'anic account (naming of Tarshish), and one detail in the Qur'anic account that is not in the biblical account (identifying of Jonah as a messenger). Then i close the chapter with some reflections on and invitations for the "commentary business," flowing from and in the interests of the EBC project (and similarly committed projects).

---

1. The background of these questions is the explanation for why Yhwh told Jonah to go to Nineveh—because their wickedness has come up before him (Jon. 1.2).

9. A Flight That Continues
117

Tarshish or bust

Jonah's response to his call was to flee to Tarshish away from the presence of YHWH, and this response is significant enough that the biblical narrator mentions it three times in the same verse (Jon. 1.3). Because it is a "distant port," it makes sense that Jonah fled to Tarshish. Tarshish is a destination far away from his home ground and his people, and from the presence of YHWH. It is so far away that Jonah needed a boat to get there which, to my islander mind, indicates that Tarshish was too far away for him to swim across or to take a raft.[2]

Rafting was common in the old days throughout Pasifika. Islanders used rafts constructed with logs and coconuts to cross between islands. In Tonga, rafts were used to cross nearby islands, for example, between 'Eua and Tongatapu, a distance of 36 kilometres/22 miles across the open sea (these islands are considered to be *close to each other* because one can see the other island on the horizon). And on some occasions, people used rafts between distant islands such as 'Ata and Tongatapu, a distance of 165 kilometres/102 miles, before and after the Peruvian slave traders (blackbirders) took over 170 people from 'Ata in the 1860s.[3] The affirmation that "our ancestors were navigators" applies to many who voyaged on rafts, with the structure and condition of their vessels highlighting their skills and stamina. There were canoes and outriggers with sails in Pasifika as well, and those were used for crossing longer distances and fearsome seas for convivial as well as colonial agendas. From the rafting and voyaging contexts of Pasifika, i read the need for a boat to reach Tarshish as evidence of how far it was from Joppa and how fierce the sea was.

In the island experience, in the modern time, boats to far away islands are less frequent and they are often cancelled. In this context i wonder if it was by chance that there was a boat to Tarshish when Jonah reached the port at Joppa, or if Tarshish was a popular and major port that there were frequent and regular services there. Linking the boat to Tarshish raises attention because boats of Tarshish are associated with power and trade (Ezek. 27.25; Isa. 2.16; Ps. 48.7), similar to the ones that Solomon used for his imperial naval force and trade (see 1 Kings 5). In this regard Jonah did not board just any boat; he boarded one of the boats that was among the fleet that goes to Tarshish. It would have been a sound and "business

---

2. On the other hand, in terms of the narrative Tarshish is *literally close by* in the eyes of readers. Readers have no excuse but to *see Tarshish* because it is named three times in the same verse (Jon. 1.3).

3. The Peruvian slave trade reached Tonga around 1862–64 and took natives from 'Ata (the southernmost island in the Tonga group) and Niua Fo'ou (to the north, closer to Samoa than to Tongatapu), but did not succeed in its attempt at 'Uiha (in the Ha'apai group). Regarding rafting and the island of 'Ata, one of the natives (Taulani) who escaped from the blackbirders rafted from 'Ata to Tongatapu to report what happened. In response Tupou I (Taufa'ahau) sent vessels to bring the remaining natives (of around 200) from 'Ata and resettled them at 'Eua (in Ha'atu'a/Kolomaile settlements) and Tongatapu.

class" vessel, and the cargo that the crew threw overboard (Jon. 1.5) were probably meant for trade and profit. Jonah would have travelled among traders as well as professional people who were business-minded, thus making sense of the second question that the mariners posed: "What is your occupation?"[4] (Jon. 1.8, NRSV). The mariners saw Jonah as a professional,[5] and i imagine that that would be a standard question to ask travellers on deck of the fleet to Tarshish.

The ships of Tarshish are also presented in positive lights: they were also expected to bring the exiles back to Jerusalem (Isa. 60.9). Something good can come from the fleet of Tarshish, but this does not rule out the not-so-good things. Vessels of exploitation and pilfering could also rescue and deliver, and vice versa. Among the fleet of Tarshish, Jonah boarded a boat that was an arcade as well as a sanctuary. The boat cannot be moored to only one "port," and so this reading floats the boat into the waters of the fish (as i proposed in Chapter 7) and under the shadows of Job: we receive the good as well as the bad from the boat (to appropriate his question in Job 2.10).

Through the events of reading forward and reading backward i engaged the workings of fantasy in the Jonah narrative and here i pause to wonder what Tarshish (as a destination) contributes to the fancy of the narrative. While the primary reason for Jonah's flight is to get away from the presence of Yhwh, the three times that Tarshish is named in Jon. 1.3 reads like a strong signal that it was significant for the narrative.[6] Some readers may react with approval that Jonah has chosen an appropriate destination, and others may react with some reservation because of the capitalist legacy of the place. On the latter, there would have been some wickedness in the place but those did not catch the attention of Yhwh.

What if there were other boats at Joppa and Jonah picked the one that was going to Tarshish? In other words, what if Jonah was intentional about reaching Tarshish? Did Jonah have anything to trade, or was he looking for something to acquire? My questions are speculative, of course, but they take advantage of the Qur'an's silence about from whom or from what Jonah ran away. There is no anxiety in the Qur'an for Jonah to get away from someone or something, but that he gets somewhere;[7] and the biblical version names his destination as Tarshish. Jonah's flight was not

4. This is the kind of question that travellers are asked when they try to cross or enter international borders.

5. For an image of Jonah as a professional and business person, see *Jonah and the Whale* (oil on board) by Fred Aris (this artwork is reproduced in Brent A. Strawn's "Jonah and Genre" https://global.oup.com/obso/focus/focus_on_jonah/).

6. One of the island experiences behind this reading is the expectation that three rainbows appearing in the sky (which is not unusual in Pasifika's water world) convey multiple messages. Natives have different understandings of what the messages are, depending on their situation, but the emphasis of this viewpoint is that the sky says more than one message.

7. While the Qur'an is also silent about Tarshish as Jonah's destination, it is certain that Jonah boarded a boat in order to go somewhere.

9. A Flight That Continues 119

aimless. He may not have had anything or means to trade, but he was going to the kind of place that has energy to make people take chances. Joseph officiated at such a place (Gen. 41.46-9), and it was there also that he took advantage of his brothers and family (Genesis 42).[8] At the open square of such places of trade and negotiation, foreigners and strangers get harassed (see Gen. 19.1-11 and Judg. 19.16-21). Then again, it is at such public places that some people have an opportunity to let go of their burdens (which is the goal of *fakatomala*, repentance; see Chapter 6). This was the case for the unnamed next-of-kin (redeemer) in Ruth 4.

The next-of-kin was anticipated the night before (Ruth 3.13) and the restless Boaz pulled him into the story the next day and presented him with a business transaction (Ruth 4.1-6): Naomi was planning to sell the land that belonged to Elimelech, and Boaz gave the next-of-kin the first chance to redeem or refuse the family inheritance. Immediately, the next-of-kin accepted. Boaz then added a twist that proved to be too much for the next-of-kin: in redeeming the inheritance of Elimelech, he must also acquire Ruth the Moabite. Because of this added condition, the next-of-kin promptly but firmly changed his mind and handed over the right to redeem to Boaz: "Then I cannot redeem it for myself, lest I impair my own estate. You take over my right of redemption, for I am unable to exercise it" (Ruth 4.6, NJPS). The trade between the next-of-kin and Boaz took place at the gate to the town, a place similar to "the opening" where Tamar sat to negotiate with Judah (Gen. 38.12-19). I imagine such places at Tarshish, and assume that Jonah knew of the energy in those places to make people do extraordinary things. In these intersections, it is possible that Jonah went to Tarshish in order to drop the burden (as in *fakatomala*) of the word of YHWH which suddenly (and uninvitedly) happened upon him. Jonah was running away *from the presence* of YHWH when he boarded the boat at Joppa, and i imagine that upon reaching Tarshish he would look for a way and a place where he would drop his burden (the word of YHWH). In this reading, if Jonah had a prayer as he boarded the boat, it would have been along the line of "let this cup pass from me" (cf. Mt. 26.39).

The proposed reading credits Jonah as a thoughtful and determined character who has reached "self-actualization" (Lacocque and Lacocque 1990: 173–94; compare with a stubborn Jonah in Perry 2006: 141 and a converted Jonah in Jenson 2008: 69–73), and raises questions around YHWH's all-out effort to stop the boat from reaching Tarshish (and as a consequence made Tarshish a forbidden site). I affirmed in the previous chapters the obvious and popular readings that YHWH's intention was to stop Jonah's flight so that he would go *to Nineveh*. Since YHWH allowed other biblical characters to walk away and even pushed some of them away from his presence (e.g. Adam, Eve, Cain, Hagar, Ishmael, Esau and ultimately,

---

8. Since the brothers betrayed Joseph earlier in the narrative (Gen. 37.12-28), one may also speak of the latter event as revenge. The risk in this alternative position is that one could overlook the power relations between Joseph (as the chief of Egypt who had authority over the storehouses) and his brothers (as victims of the famine who, being foreigners to Egypt, came looking for food).

Israel, in the exile), i do not see why Jonah's flight from Yʜᴡʜ's presence was a problem. Yʜᴡʜ could have found an alternative messenger to take Jonah's place (as he selected David to replace Saul, and Elisha came on the scene before Elijah expired). I thus stress here that Yʜᴡʜ stopped Jonah from arriving *at Tarshish*. There must have been something about Tarshish and what Jonah could do there, along the lines that i suggested above, that made Yʜᴡʜ furious and wanted to stop him from reaching Tarshish. In this connection, Yʜᴡʜ busted Jonah's flight.

From an ecological standpoint, judging on the basis of the decisions and resolutions that come from the centres of trade in the modern world, Tarshish would have been a place where the condition and health of the land, the sea and the atmosphere were not taken as priority. Yʜᴡʜ's stoppage of Jonah's flight prevented both of them from seeing and addressing the ecological impacts of trade and profiteering. Jonah's flight thus revealed something about both Tarshish and Yʜᴡʜ. Tarshish was a place of chances and breaks, and Yʜᴡʜ did not want Jonah to go there. The flight of Jonah, in return, busted Yʜᴡʜ.

Among the messengers

The Qur'an identifies Jonah as a messenger (read: prophet), but the biblical narrative does not name him as one or present him as a character who befits that designation.[9] This is not to say that messengers do not drop (as Jonah did the first time) or peak at the messages that they are given to carry.[10] Some messengers may even alter their given message(s), as i suggested in Chapter 6 (out of respect to the interests of Nineveh) concerning Jonah. These propensities, however, do not make Jonah a messenger. There are three elements to consider in light of this reflection: first, what did it mean to be or involve being a messenger; second, whether Jonah was or looked like a messenger; and third, whether Jonah wanted to be or accepted being a messenger. In the interest of Jonah, i lay more emphasis on the third element.

Both the Qur'an and the Hebrew Bible (by putting the Jonah narrative in the book of the Twelve, among the *Nevi'im*/prophets) seek to make Jonah a messenger or prophet, and generations of biblical critics have added their weight to conceive him as one.[11] But Jonah the biblical character did not want to be a messenger. While the words of Yʜᴡʜ *happened* to and troubled him, that did not make him a

---

9. Jonah is in the same boat as Abram, Sarai, Hagar and most of the women in the Bible upon whom the words of Yʜᴡʜ happened but are not seen as messengers or prophet(esse)s.

10. One of the ironies in the story of Uriah is that he carried a letter that gave instruction intended to get him killed (2 Sam. 11.14-15). The text does not say (but readers infer) that David sealed the letter or that Uriah actually delivered the message to Joab, so one may rightly ask if Uriah read the letter and decided not to deliver it.

11. Jacques Ellul, for instance, still concluded that the book should be read as a prophetic book despite all of its historical and religious embellishments (see Ellul 1971: 18, 37).

messenger. And even if Jon. 1.1-2 is read as a call narrative, he simply did not want to be a messenger. Period. When he boarded the boat for Tarshish, therefore, part of his burden would have been the expectation in the world of the story that he was a messenger. Put more directly, Jonah was burdened with being *forced* among the messengers (Sūrah 37.139) and, in the afterlife of the narrative, he would have been laden with the unwillingness of readers to push back at the words of YHWH. In this connection, Jonah's flight is a rejection both of the words of YHWH and of the function (or profession) of messengers.[12]

In Pasifika, to be messengers with the privilege to speak to and for one's community is highly praised and desired in both cultural and church circles.[13] Native messengers speak for their chiefs and community as well as for themselves, and this role requires people who have special oratorical skills. Similar to other oral-preferring cultures, orators in Pasifika are more than couriers. They also interpret and present (read: twist) the message for as well as negotiate with (read: persuade, manipulate) their communities or congregations (as preachers and pastors). Many Pasifika natives aspire to be orators, and they go to great lengths and expenses to gain the approval of the elders in order to join the ranks (see Tamasese 2011). Jonah, on the other hand, did not want to be in such a company, and one could argue that his story is a critique of people who pursue the inspirations of messengers. Jonah would have found such people fishy.

Jonah did not want to be a messenger, but there are interesting messages in his flight. This claim echoes the Tongan saying *tu'a e tangata kae 'eiki e fekau* (the person is a commoner, but the message is noble), which asserts that there are worthy messages even in unworthy messengers. Jonah did not fit the profile of a messenger but he had noble messages. Focusing on Jon. 1.1-3, i appreciate four noble messages in Jonah's flight.

First, in fleeing Jonah communicated a strong signal that YHWH did not have sovereignty over all lands. He fled to Tarshish because it was "away from the presence of YHWH" (Jon. 1.3) and in juxtaposition, so was Nineveh. Jonah did not reach Tarshish but his going to Nineveh was because YHWH would not go there on his own. And even though YHWH responded to Jonah's prayer in Jon. 4.1-4 (which was made within the city, as i argued in Chapter 6), there is no evidence in the whole narrative that YHWH entered Nineveh.[14] YHWH did show concern for Nineveh at the end (Jon. 4.10-11), but the narrative does not show that the great city was (converted) under YHWH's authority. Jonah's flight thus exposed geographical limits in YHWH's reign. He did not have sovereignty over *great* places like Nineveh and Tarshish.

---

12. At the hermeneutical level, Jonah's flight may also be read as a push back at the control of scripture.

13. Like other patriarchal societies, in Pasifika men have more chances than women to take up roles in cultural and church circles.

14. If the almighty YHWH had gone and spoken directly to Nineveh, he would not need Jonah to be a messenger.

122   *Jonah*

Second, the Tarshish-based explanations suggested in the previous section for why Yʜwʜ stopped Jonah from reaching Tarshish persuade the opinion that Yʜwʜ did not want to see the situation at that centre of power and trade. The incentive for this move is that, to convert a popular saying, *if monkey does not see monkey does not do*. This is a painful disposition in current contexts of climate injustice because it is an excuse to deny climate change and climate effect. It is easier to (fly over and) *not see*, and to finance projects in order to distract attention from (read: *not see*) climate injustices, than for monkey to see and be obliged to do something. In the context of Pasifika, we see many monkeys. And in the case of Tarshish, i see Yʜwʜ as one of the monkeys.

Third, in his flight Jonah joined a company of other people going to Tarshish (Jon. 1.3c). They shared the same destination, but they travelled for different purposes. I imagine some of them to have been to Tarshish previously but *did not see* the ecological conditions, or be bothered by the ecological impacts, of the land.[15] I also imagine that there would have been some exceptions so there would have been travellers who saw the conditions and responded appropriately. They too were denied the chance to interact and collaborate with Jonah. The stoppage of Jonah's flight denied readers of the chance to see the diversity of *passengers* who use the fleet of Tarshish, and Jonah of the chance to deliver a message to, or be a message for, Tarshish. What that message might have been is a riddle for readers.

Fourth, Jonah's flight was stopped from reaching Tarshish but it did not end at sea. He was swallowed then vomited by the great fish, then he walked into Nineveh and exited to continue his flight beyond the city. At the end of the narrative some words from Yʜwʜ again happened upon him (Jon. 4.10-11) and again he did not respond with a single word. In Jon. 1.3 he silently (according to the text) fled to Tarshish, and in Jon. 4.11 he silently fled into the imaginations of readers. Yʜwʜ stopped his flight from reaching Tarshish, but his flight from the presence of Yʜwʜ continues beyond the limits of texts and scriptures.

Some messages are spoken and written, and some messages come out from the gaps and silences of the spoken and the written. In the case of Jonah, there were messages even in his flight from the message of Yʜwʜ. I tried to put some of those messages into words in this section, before my own flight.

Invitations

At the end of the *reading forward* and *reading backward* exercises in this EBC study, i look back in this closing section (to this chapter as well as to this work) to the commentary business (see Chapter 1). Circling around Jonah (as narrative and as character), i highlight the following observations and invitations.

---

15. The ecological impacts of a land spread beyond its borders, and one of the challenges here is for centres of power and trade to realize that what they *do unto others* they also *do unto themselves*.

First, ending this study at the beginning of the Jonah narrative (Jon. 1.1-3) is also an invitation for readers to meander and circle in, around and beyond the text. Readings that are linear in orientation give the impression that the text is straightforward and simple, rather than also being intricate, winding, playful and queer. And even devious. With a text like the Jonah narrative, it is difficult to be straightforward and to keep a straight face. The narrative is tongue-in-cheek at several places, with several winks here and there, and the commentary business would benefit from adopting those outlooks.

Second, the subtitle to Jack Sasson's authoritative and influential commentary—*Jonah: A New Translation with Introduction, Commentary, and Interpretations* (1990)—is evidence of the biases in mainline biblical scholarship that imagine and construct disciplinary divides between *commentary* (read: exegesis) and *interpretations* (read: hermeneutics). While those biases are understandable for the academic settings prior to the 1990s, the conditions of biblical scholarship (especially under the influences of narrative, contextual, postmodern and postcolonial biblical criticisms) and of the earth(ed) have changed since then thus inviting alternative ways of "trading" (to use an image associated with Tarshish above) in the commentary business. Changes have arrived and they indeed are slowly restructuring the commentary business. Framed in terms of contextual interpretation, Athalya Brenner-Idan is among biblical critics who welcome the change of paradigms and methodologies in the commentary business:

> Contextual interpretation adds a blow to the pretense of interpreter's objectivity; it upsets social (including gender) and geographical hegemonies; it decentralizes and de-marginalizes both the biblical texts and their readers; it refreshes default choices for text criticism and commentary. In short, a change. A welcome change. (Brenner-Idan 2016: 1)

Welcoming the opportunities in and to change, this EBC study went back to and through the Jonah narratives (in the Hebrew Bible and the Qur'an) as well as forward to current situations outside of the canonical texts, driven by concerns for the ecological conditions of the earth(ed) and the challenges of climate injustice. In the eyes of mainline biblical scholarship, this EBC study would appear as if it is a flight away from the commentary business. It is nonetheless a flight that *lands* at the intersections of what Sasson understood as *commentary* (or exegesis) and *interpretations* (or hermeneutics). It lands on the grounds of the mainline commentary business, but it does not come to rest there.

This study is completely interested and i hope that it encourages other interested readers to also "invest" in the commentary business. To read ancient texts with and for *interests* sometimes requires readers to resist the texts and their plots. Doing so frees readers from ancient mindsets, to become rooted in the present and to anticipate the future (and to engage the mindsets that percolate at those intersections). Concerning the commentary business, i suggest that its future depends not solely on what ancient texts said but also on what ancient texts hear in the concerns and struggles of the times. In both cases, there is much to trade between ancient texts, interested and rooted readers, and the future that awaits in life's roots (appealing to Donet's works, see Figures 1.1 and 1.2) and routes (appealing to the heritage of Pasifika voyagers). Here at this juncture, i quickly add that preoccupation with the future (or the world to come) is as problematic as being stuck in the past (ancient, history). Caveat lector. It is vital for readers to be attentive to the past and future without losing sight of the present, so that we may *see and do* responsibly (see also De La Torre 2007) in light of the conditions and politics of climate change.

Third, in this EBC study i took advantage of the (obvious) energies of fantasy and fabrication in the Jonah narratives, to see the story take flight from the limits of textuality and the controls of scriptures. I imagined myself entering (as a native reader) the world of the narrative but i did not seek to verify, justify or repent it. Rather, i surfed the flows of the narrative in order to engage the narrator and the characters, and at places got sucked into the queer and satirical tones of the narrative and/or was carried away in the hermeneutical rip that comes with reading across cultures.

In this chapter I focused on Jonah's flight for several reasons: because the story involves a flight over several stages and it did not end in the text;[16] because the story is in canons that have the power to make the unprophetic prophetic, the unreal real and the unmovable move; because, appealing to Sasson's distinction, ancient texts take flight at the intersections of commentary and interpretations, in other words, readers make ancient texts fly; and because this is one way to make the text hear the current situations of climate change and climate injustice. I followed the story in its flight over several paths, and i tried to *land* it at the stormy shores of life and living.

Fourth, i used the oral-preferring *talanoa* (story, telling of story, conversation around story and telling) approach to retell the same story over and over again, forward as well as backward, with a different twist each time. Repetition and reconsideration are marks of *talanoa*, and they are ongoing. Moving. In flight. But they also land. At places. Real places. Legendary places. Narrative places. Then they take off again. And again. So *talanoa* is never complete(d). I propose those *talanoa* qualities for the commentary business, and highlight some of their evidences and implications in the following paragraphs.

I found the Jonah story telling itself as well as engaging other stories outside of my interests and influence. For instance, in identifying Jonah as "son of Amittai" (Jon. 1.1) the story locates itself in the shadows of 2 Kgs 14.23-9 and the time of Jeroboam II (on this intertextual link, see Muldoon 2010: 102–21). And with Nineveh as its primary focus the story engages with, as well as provides a countering voice against, the book of Nahum (see Vance 2011). The story (*talanoa*) on its own

---

16. Jesus helped keep Jonah in flight by associating his three days and three nights in the belly of the great fish with death, and then releasing Jonah into the world of the resurrected (Mt. 12.40). In this regard, the Qur'anic version is respectful (and may have been aware) of Jesus's view.

tells (*talanoa*) itself in light of these intertextual hints and initiates conversations (*talanoa*) with them no matter whether i noticed or emphasized them or not (and i did not). Put simply, *talanoa* takes place without my influence.

Notwithstanding, i also contributed to the *talanoa* events in the sense that my readings made the story restless so that it, to borrow the experience of the great fish, spewed other meanings and purposes. In this chapter, through *talanoa*, i assisted Jonah in his flight and extended his flight beyond the limits of the text. But unlike the great fish, *talanoa* did not die after spilling the story. As long as story, telling and conversation take place, with or without my or other readers' influence, *talanoa* murmurs and ripples. And as long as there are excesses and riddles in the story for other readers, the story too does not die.[17] Given those readerly occasions, the events of *talanoa* are clearly not innocent. Those events enabled me to enter the world of the narrative, to return to the time and home of our ancestors, and to *see and do* many other things.

Talanoa problematizes the desires for certainty and finality that circulate in the mainline commentary business, and thus frees the text from my control as reader. This is a humbling confession because it makes me recognize the right of other readers to find and defend other readings, and reminds me that i do not have the final say in determining the meanings and functions of the story. Deliverance belongs to the story!

Fifth, in part because this is an EBC work and in part because of my own backgrounds and orientations, i appealed to native experiences and insights to make the Jonah narratives *come up in the presence of* the land, the sea, the underworld and their many hosts. In doing so i have woven a proverbial mat (see pp. 14–16) large enough for Jonah, Yhwh, the narrator, the beasts, the bush, the earth(ed) and other subjects who have met and engaged in these pages.

Returning to the commentary business, with native and EBC twists, commentary-and-interpretation is more than attempts to make texts talk so that voices from the past may speak in(to) the present; it is also about enabling texts (written and oral) and subjects (embodied and imagined) to hear each other and to engage in *talanoa*. It is common and easier to hear voices from the past; the challenge is to also make subjects from the past hear the voices and cries in and

---

17. One of the notable excesses not discussed in this work is *The Tales of the Prophets of al-Kisa'i* (see translation in Limburg 1993: 115–18) with its additional twists and turns: Jonah fled with his family; Allah took his family and possessions away, thinking that they were the reason why Jonah did not want to do His will; for forty days Jonah preached, "confess that there is no god but Allah and that I, Jonah, am His servant and messenger," but the people did not believe him; Allah told Jonah to leave the city, and sent Gabriel to summon Malik, who rained sparks on the city; the city believed and repented; Jonah was angry and he fled on a boat; a storm came, and then a fish from India opened its mouth for Jonah to jump in; out of the fish and after the bush event Jonah found his wife, his wealth and his sons; they returned as a family to his own city, and before he died he encouraged his people to do justice and to refrain from evil.

from the present[18]—this is one of the "radical re-orientation[s] to the biblical text" (Habel) that i have attempted in this EBC offering.

Sixth, tweaking the basic definition of exegesis (favoured in the mainline sector of the commentary business) as to *lead out* meanings that are in the text, i close this EBC study with an invitation for commentators to then *let go* of the text and the meanings that they have made to come out from the text. In the Jonah narrative, some characters would find the invitation to *let go* easy. To let go of the words of YHWH was easy for Jonah. He ran away to a boat. To let go of the cargo for Tarshish was easy for the mariners. They rubbished the sea. To let go of their evil ways was easy for Nineveh. They fasted and changed their ways. To let go of his opinion concerning Nineveh was easy for YHWH. He repented. To let go of its human snack was easy for the great fish. It vomited. To let go of the need to respond to YHWH's closing statement was easy for Jonah. He was silent.

Among those that let go, this work i also let go.

---

18. Along this line, see the discussion of the "Pitfalls Jonah Should Avoid" and "Case Studies: What Would Jonah Do?" by De La Torre (2007: 123–65).

A POSTSCRIPT

An afterthought, at the invitation of Norman Habel: What are steps for *reading forward* and *reading backward* biblical narratives?

I identify and introduce several steps around four platforms: preparation, plotting (reading forward), passing (reading backward) and privileging (reading for). Because reading for me is similar to surfing, the following depictions come at the intersection of surf and turf. I depict these platforms in light of what i have done with Jonah, and you may surf or shuffle as you deem appropriate for your (is)land- and sea-scapes.

Preparation

Reading biblical texts is a dish best served with open minds, but this does not mean that we are innocent when we read biblical texts. So, prepare to read and be upfront that we have biases and commitments. And let us not be naive about the texts' politics and interests.

The following reminders usually prepare me to read:

- Every wave has at least two sides—a (face) side that breaks or rolls and a (back) side that rides or rests—and every wave is different. So are biblical texts, and as a reader i prepare to present as many sides of the texts as i could see.
- In the sea, currents move in many directions. So are the currents (energies, concerns) in and of biblical texts. They are not linear, nor straightforward.
- Waves break onto shore and the water ripple away from the shoreline, out to the open. So do texts break and ripple away, away from the control of readers.
- Pick the wave(s) to surf. In this work, i focused on three waves—the Jonah narrative, climate change and the commentary business—and the ripples of those waves took me into deep waters.
- Prepare to take water or swim (*when*, not if, the text throws you off). In other words, prepare to fail—which is something for which Jonah was not prepared. On the other hand, when Nineveh repented "the city" accepted that "they failed."
- No one lives in the world of the biblical text, and no one can live in the sea forever.

These reminders set the tone and stir the desire to read *and reread*. The stronger the desire to reread, the more creative one becomes in orienting the direction of one's reading to the point when it becomes possible to "carve" (the term for turning on a wave) the text. When one could turn and surf against the power of the text, one is prepared to read the narrative forward as well as to read it backward.

Plotting

This is the platform for *reading forward*, and i use "plotting" as a reminder that honouring the plot of the narrative requires one to buy into the plotting of the narrator. This is one way of saying that the narrator and the text are not innocent or naive.

- How does the narrative open? In Jonah's case, he turned his back on the words of YHWH. Jonah's flight is the "strong current" at the opening of the narrative, and as i read forward (and backward) i watch out for how it collides with other currents.
- How does the narrative flow, or what is the orientation of the narrative? This question points in two directions:
  - The physical or bodied (albeit storied) flow of the narrative: the Jonah narrative flows into the sea, the fish, the city, then outside of Nineveh.
  - The ideological flow of the narrative: Did Jonah change his mind about the words of YHWH? He walked into Nineveh, but that did not mean that he approved the words of YHWH (some people do things that they don't even approve). And he ended up outside of Nineveh, but the "words of YHWH" did not leave Nineveh behind. What are other ideological flows in the narrative?

- What other "currents" emerge in and affect the flow of the narrative? A significant current for my reading is the repentance of Nineveh (city, people and beasts), which influenced YHWH into repentance. Of significance also are the voices and impacts of earth(ed) subjects. How do other currents run into the strong current at the opening of the narrative?
- How does the narrative end?

  - Physical end: outside of Nineveh.
  - Ideological end: inside of Nineveh.

With the insights that those questions bring up, *read forward* through the narrative and take note of places (especially where textual currents collide) where the narrative "swells" (fractures or tensions in the narrative that swirls with extra meanings). Those swells are markers for *reading backward*.

A Postscript 129

Passing

This is the platform for *reading backward*, and i use "passing" because this is where i "pass on" the narrator's plotting. Passing on the biblical narrator is easy because i do not live in the world of the biblical text and besides, the biblical text is not native to my world. As a consequence, i was intentional in bringing "native texts" to run into (and sometimes collide) with the biblical narrator's plotting. There are three steps for reading backward:

- Recall the swells in the *reading forward*, and how those collide with the narrator's plot: in my case, i was drawn to the repeated references to Tarshish, the state of the boat, the cargo overboard, the great fish that was supposed to be calm and obedient, the runagate who prayed to the being from whom he fled, Nineveh as city of God, beasts that fasted, a bush that was magical, a death-wishing debater, and a stubbornly patient Yнwн.
- Read those swells backward through two lines:
  - Physical line
    - Starting from the end of the narrative, nominate points of focus: in my case, i opted for the "number 2s"—beasts, bush, city, fish, boat and Jonah's failed flight.
    - Determine the limits of each "swell" (read: unit, which may not be the same as in the *reading forward* process) on account of the points of focus.
    - Read the unit so that it is not trapped by the narrator's plotting.
  - Ideological line
    - Starting from the end of the narrative, focus on the alternative currents and explore how those intersect or collide with the strong(er) currents in the narrator's plot. For instance, what changed the mind of Yнwн? What could happen to the fish after it vomited?
    - Read backward from other scriptures (e.g. Qur'an) and other "texts" (e.g. Pasifika customs and legends).
- As you read backward, *curve* the textual swells/units in order to add something to the narrator's plotting.

In *reading backward* one's orientation flows against the narrator's plotting. This is what old-line biblical scholarship calls eisegesis, a methodological sin in the eyes of the academy. The *curving* question here is obvious: Is exegesis possible without eisegesis?

Privileging

Whether one reads forward or reads backward, reading is a privileging exercise; and privileging is a drill that discriminates. It thus makes sense to read in both directions, to flow with both orientations, forward and backward.

REFERENCES

Amit, Yairah. (2001). *Reading Biblical Narratives*. Minneapolis: Fortress.

Anderson, Gary A. and Markus Bockmuehl, eds (2018). *Creation* ex nihilo: *Origins, Development, Contemporary Challenges*. Notre Dame: University of Notre Dame Press.

Avalos, Hector. (2007). *The End of Biblical Studies*. Amherst, NY: Prometheus.

Ben Zvi, Ehud. (2003). *Signs of Jonah: Reading and Rereading in Ancient Yehud*. JSOTS 367. Sheffield: Sheffield Academic.

Berger, Yitzak. (2016). *Jonah in the Shadows of Eden*. Bloomington and Indianapolis: Indiana University Press.

Boase, Elizabeth and Sarah Agnew. (2016). '"Whispered in the Sound of Silence": Traumatising the Book of Jonah'. *Bible and Critical Theory* 12: 4–22.

Bob, Steven. (2013). *Go to Nineveh: Medieval Jewish Commentaries on the Book of Jonah*. Eugene: Pickwick.

Bolin, Thomas M. (1997). *Freedom Beyond Forgiveness: The Book of Jonah Re-examined*. JSOTS 236. Sheffield: Sheffield Academic.

Brenner-Idan, Athalya. (2016). 'So Where Are We? Some Reflections on Contextual Interpretation as Practiced'. A paper delivered at the Society of Biblical Literature International Meeting. Seoul, South Korea (4 July).

Carden, Michael. (2006). 'The Book of the Twelve Minor Prophets'. In *The Queer Bible Commentary*, edited by Deryn Guest, Robert E. Goss, Mona West and Thomas Bohache, 432–84. London: SCM Press.

Caspi, Mishael M. and John T. Greene, eds (2011). *How Jonah Is Interpreted in Judaism, Christianity, and Islam: Essays on the Authenticity and Influence of the Biblical Prophet*. Lewiston: Edwin Mellen.

Chen, Nan Jou. (2004). 'Jonah'. In *Global Bible Commentary*, edited by Daniel Patte et al., 291–4. Nashville: Abingdon Press.

Clines, David J. A. (1995). 'The Ten Commandments: Reading from Left to Right'. In *Words Remembered, Texts Renewed*, Fest. John F. A. Sawyer, edited by Jon Davies, Graham Harvey, Wilfred G. E. Watson, 97–112. Sheffield: Sheffield Academic Press.

Clines, David J. A. (1998). 'Reading Esther from Left to Right: Contemporary Strategies for Reading a Biblical Text'. In *On the Way to the Postmodern: Old Testament Essays, 1967–1998*, edited by David J. A. Clines, 3–22. Sheffield: Sheffield Academic Press.

Cohn, Gabriël. (1969). *Das Buch Jonä im lichte der Biblischen Erzählkunst*. Assen: Van Gorcum.

Cones, Bryan and Stephen Burns. (2019). 'Introduction: The Vivid Richness of God's Image'. In *Liturgy with a Difference: Beyond Inclusion in the Christian Assembly*, edited by Stephen Burns and Bryan Cones, xiii–xix. London: SCM Press.

Craig, Kenneth M., Jr. (1993). *A Poetics of Jonah: Art in the Service of Ideology*. Columbia: University of South Carolina Press.

Davidson, Steed Vernyl. (2015). 'Shifting Readings of Genesis 38 and Daniel 8'. In *Islands, Islanders and the Bible: RumInations*, edited by Jione Havea, Margaret Aymer and Steed Vernyl Davidson, 37–56. Atlanta: SBL.

De La Torre, Miguel A. (2007). *Liberating Jonah: Forming an Ethics of Reconciliation*. Maryknoll: Orbis.

De La Torre, Miguel A. (2019a). *Burying White Privilege: Resurrecting a Badass Christianity*. Grand Rapids: Eerdmans.

De La Torre, Miguel A. (2019b). 'Worship through Sanctuary'. In *Liturgy with a Difference: Beyond Inclusion in the Christian Assembly*, edited by Stephen Burns and Bryan Cones, 154–64. London: SCM Press.

Douglas, Mary. (1966). *Purity and Danger: An Analysis of Concepts of Pollution and Taboo*. New York: Routledge.

Dube, Musa. (1998). '"Go Therefore and Make Disciples of All Nations" (Matt 28:19a). A Postcolonial Perspective on Biblical Criticism and Pedagogy'. In *Teaching the Bible: The Discourses and Politics of Biblical Pedagogy*, edited by Fernando F. Segovia and Mary A. Tolbert, 224–46. New York: Orbis.

Edwards, Denis. (2006). *Ecology at the Heart of Faith: The Change of Heart That Leads to a New Way of Living on Earth*. Maryknoll, NY: Orbis.

Ellul, Jacques. (1971). *The Judgment of Jonah*. Grand Rapids: Eerdmans.

Fa'aleava, Milo Toleafoa. (1983). 'Unity in Diversity in the Book of Jonah'. MTh thesis, Pacific Theological College, Suva, Fiji.

Fewell, Danna Nolan. (2003). *The Children of Israel: Reading the Bible for the Sake of Our Children*. Nashville: Abingdon.

Gaines, Janet Howe. (2003). *Forgiveness in a Wounded World: Jonah's Dilemma*. Atlanta: Society of Biblical Literature.

Gruber, Mayer I. (2001). 'Nineveh the Adulteress'. In *Prophets and Daniel: A Feminist Companion to the Bible (Second Series)*, edited by Athalya Brenner, 220–5. Sheffield: Sheffield Academic Press.

Gunn, David M. (1980). *The Fate of King Saul: An Interpretation of a Biblical Story*. Sheffield: JSOT.

Habel, Norman. (2011). *The Birth, the Curse and the Greening of Earth: An Ecological Reading of Genesis 1–11*. Sheffield: Sheffield Phoenix Press.

Haluk, Markus. (2017). *Dead or Alive: The Loss of Hopes and Human Rights in Papua*. Jayapura, West Papua: Deiyai Publishing.

Handy, Lowell K. (2007). *Jonah's World: Social Science and the Reading of Prophetic Story*. London: Equinox.

Havea, Jione. (2004). 'Would the Real Native Please Sit Down!' In *Faith in a Hyphen: Cross-Cultural Theologies Down Under*, edited by Clive Pearson, 199–210, 254–6. Parramatta and Adelaide: UTC Publications and Openbook.

Havea, Jione. (2007). 'Is There a Home for the Bible in the Postmodern World?' *Journal of Ecumenical Studies* 42.4 (Fall): 547–59.

Havea, Jione, ed. (2018a). *Power and Religion*. Lanham: Lexington Books/Fortress Academics.

Havea, Jione, ed. (2018b). *Sea of Readings: The Bible and the South Pacific*. Atlanta: SBL Press.

Havea, Jione. (2019a). 'The Land Has Colours'. In *People and Land*, edited by Jione Havea. Lanham: Lexington Books/Fortress Academics (forthcoming).

Havea, Jione, ed. (2019b). *Scripture and Resistance*. Lanham: Lexington Books/Fortress Academics.

Havea, Jione and Monica J. Melanchthon. (2016). 'Culture Tricks in Biblical Narrative'. In *The Oxford Handbook of Biblical Narrative*, edited by Danna Nolan Fewell, 563–72. New York: Oxford University Press.

References

Havea, Jione and Peter H. W. Lau. (forthcoming). 'Context Matters: Reading from Asia and Pasifika.' In *Reading Ecclesiastes from Asia and Pasifika*, edited by Jione Havea and Peter H. W. Lau. Atlanta: SBL Press.

Havea, Jione, Margaret O. Aymer and Steed Davidson, eds (2015). *Islands, Islanders, and Bible: RumInations*. Atlanta: SBL Press.

Hedrick, Charles W. (2004). *Many Things in Parables: Jesus and His Modern Critics*. Louisville: Westminster John Knox.

Hereniko, Vilisoni. (2004). *The Land Has Eyes*. Suva: Te Maka Productions.

Jagessar, Michael. (2018). 'Chanting Down the Shitstem—Resistance with Anasi and Rastafari Optics'. In *Religion and Power*, edited by Jione Havea, 87–104. Langham: Lexington Books/Fortress Academic.

Jenson, Philip Peter. (2008). *Obadiah, Jonah, Micah: A Theological Commentary*. New York: t&t clark.

Jobling, David. (1998). *1 Samuel*. A Michael Glazier Book. Collegeville: Liturgical)

Ka'ili, Tevita O. (2005). '*Tauhi vā*: Nurturing Tongan Sociospatial Ties in Maui and Beyond'. *The Contemporary Pacific* 17: 83–114.

Kamp, Albert. (2004). *Inner Worlds: A Cognitive Linguistic Approach to the Book of Jonah*. Boston and Leiden: Brill Academic.

Kim, Heup Young. (2017). *A Theology of Dao*. Maryknoll: Orbis Books.

Kunz-Lübcke, Andreas. (2016). 'Jonah, Robinsons and Unlimited Gods: Re-reading Jonah as a Sea Adventure Story'. *Bible and Critical Theory* 12: 62–78.

LaCocque, Andre and Pierre-Emmanuel LaCocque. (1990). *Jonah. A Psycho-Religious Approach to the Prophet*. Columbia: University of South Carolina Press.

Lasine, Stuart. (2016). 'Jonah's Complexes and Our Own: Psychology and the Interpretation of the Book of Jonah'. *Journal for the Study of the Old Testament* 41.2: 237–60.

Limburg, James. (1993). *Jonah: A Commentary*. OTL. Louisville: Westminster/John Knox.

Lindsay, Rebecca. (2016). 'Overthrowing Nineveh: Revisiting the City with Postcolonial Imagination'. *Bible and Critical Theory* 12: 49–61.

MacLeod, Jason. (2015). *Merdeka and the Morning Star: Civil Resistance in West Papua*. Peace and Conflict Series, St. Lucia: University of Queensland Press.

Magonet, Jonathan. (1983). *Form and Meaning: Studies in Literary Techniques in the Book of Jonah*. Sheffield: Almond.

March, Stephen John. (2014). *Jonah – The Epistle of Wild Grace*. UK: Lulu.

McKenzie, Steven L. (2005). *How to Read the Bible: History, Prophecy, Literature—Why Modern Readers Need to Know the Difference, and What It Means for Faith Today*. New York: Oxford University Press.

Muldoon, Catherine L. (2010). *In Defense of Divine Justice: An Intertextual Approach to the Book of Jonah*. Washington: Catholic Biblical Association of America.

Nicole, Eugenia. (1990). 'Jonah: An Invitation to Dialogue'. MTh Thesis, Pacific Theological College, Suva, Fiji.

Perry, T. A. (2006). *The Honeymoon Is Over: Jonah's Argument with God*. Peabody: Hendrickson.

Person, Raymond F., Jr. (1996). *In Conversation with Jonah: Conversation Analysis, Literary Criticism, and the Book of Jonah*. JSOTS 220. Sheffield: Sheffield Academic.

Proctor, Mark A. (2019). '"Who Is My Neighbor?": Recontextualizing Luke's Good Samaritan (Luke 10:25–37)'. *JBL* 138: 203–19.

Rieger, Joerg. (2007). *Christ & Empire: From Paul to Postcolonial Times*. Minneapolis, MN: Augsburg Fortress.

Sasson, Jack M. (1990). *Jonah: A New Translation with Introduction, Commentary, and Interpretations*. Anchor Bible 24B. New York: Doubleday.

Scott, James C. (1990). *Domination and the Arts of Resistance: Hidden Transcripts*. New Haven: Yale University Press.

Shemesh, Yael. (2010). "'And Many Beasts' (Jonah 4:11): The Function and Status of Animals in the Book of Jonah'. *The Journal of Hebrew Scriptures* 10.6: 2–26.

Sherwood, Yvonne. (2000). *A Biblical Text and Its Afterlives. The Survival of Jonah in Western Culture*. Cambridge: Cambridge University Press.

Simon, Uriel. (1999). *The JPS Bible Commentary: Jonah*. Trans. Lenn J. Schramm. Philadelphia: Jewish Publication Society.

Tamasese, Tusi. (2011). *O Le Tulafale [The Orator]*. Auckland: Transmission Films.

Timmer, Daniel C. (2011). *A Gracious and Compassionate God: Mission, Salvation and Spirituality in the Book of Jonah*. Downers Grove: InterVarsity.

Tupou-Thomas, Sisilia. (2004). 'Telling Tales'. In *Faith in a Hyphen: Cross-Cultural Theologies Down Under*, edited by Clive Pearson, 1–4. Adelaide: Openbooks.

Vaka'uta, Nāsili. (2014). 'A Tongan Island Reading of Jonah as Oriented Towards the Ocean'. In *Global Perspectives on the Bible*, edited by Mark Roncace and Joseph Weaver, 128–9. Boston: Prentice Hall.

Vance, Donad R. (2011). '*Jonah* in the Mirror of *Nahum*'. In *How Jonah Is Interpreted in Judaism, Christianity, and Islam: Essays on the Authenticity and Influence of the Biblical Prophet*, edited by Mishael M. Caspi and John T. Greene, 155–70. Lewiston: Edwin Mellen.

Ward, James M. (1991). *Thus Says the Lord: The Message of the Prophets*. Nashville: Abingdon.

West, Gerald O. (2014). 'Juxtaposing 'Many Cattle' in Biblical Narrative (Jonah 4:11), Imperial Narrative, Neo-indigenous Narrative'. *Old Testament Essays* 27.2: 722–51 (http://www.scielo.org.za/scielo.php?script=sci_arttext&pid=S1010-99192014000200023).

West, Gerald O. (2019). 'Scripture as a Site of Struggle: Literary and Socio-historical Resources for Prophetic Theology in Post-colonial, Post-apartheid (Neo-colonial?) South Africa'. In *Scripture and Resistance*, edited by Jione Havea, 149–63. Lanham: Lexington Books/Fortress Academics.

White, Lynn, Jr. (1967). 'The Historical Roots of Our Ecological Crisis'. *Science* 155.3767: 1203–7.

White, Marsha C. (1992). 'Jonah'. In *The Women's Bible Commentary*, edited by Carol A. Newsom and Sharon H. Ringe, 212–14. Louisville: Westminster/John Knox.

Wiliame, Geraldine Varea. (2017). '*Fara*: A Dance of Calming the Sea of Religious Turmoil in Jonah 1'. MTh Thesis, Pacific Theological College, Suva, Fiji.

Wolff, Hans Walter. (1977). *Obadiah and Jonah: A Commentary*. Trans. Margaret Kohl. Minneapolis: Augsburg.

Yee, Gale. (2003). *Poor Banished Children of Eve: Woman as Evil in the Hebrew Bible*. Minneapolis: Augsburg/Fortress.

Youngblood, Kevin J. (2013). *Jonah: God's Scandalous Mercy*. Grand Rapids: Zondervan.

SCRIPTURAL CHARACTERS INDEX*

Aaron 83
Abel 58 n.4
Abraham 38, 39, 84, 97, 98, 101
  Abram 63, 98, 101, 120 n.9
adam (Adam) 20, 48, 58, 62, 64, 106,
  119
adamah (ha'adamah) 20, 57
  ground (אדמה) 16, 19–22, 39, 45 n.4,
    48, 57, 58 n.4, 94
Amalekite 89
Amittai 19, 20, 124
Amorites 101
ass, Balaam's 106
Assyria(n) 8, 21, 87, 97

Babel 78, 81
Babylon 8, 95
Balaam 106
Bathsheba 71
Behemoth 58–61, 62, 82, 94
Ben-Oni (Benjamin) 102
Bethlehem 98–9, 101–2
b'hemah (beasts, cattle) 56–8, 61–4
Boaz 102, 119

Cain 39, 58 n.4, 78, 119
calf, golden 46, 83–4
Canaan(ites) 19, 37, 39, 81, 88, 101
cattle, *see b'hemah*
Chilion 98–9

daughters (Nephilim) 82
David 2, 37, 39, 71, 102 n.12, 120
deep, the 5, 29, 30, 31, 32, 33, 57, 94,
  99, 100, 109, 127
Dinah 71

ears of grain 94
Egypt(ian) 37, 39, 47, 64, 83, 84, 97, 98,
  101, 119 n.8
Elijah 120
Elimelech 98, 119
Elisha 120
Ephrath 101
Erets 56, 57 n.3
Esau 64, 119
Eve 106, 119
Ezekiel 89

fools 94

Gabriel 125 n.17
Girgashites 101

Hagar 47, 98, 101, 119, 120 n.9
Hittites 101

innkeeper, the 74
Isaac 84, 97, 98, 101
Ishmael 98, 101, 119
Israel 8, 19–21, 28, 37–9, 45, 47, 49,
  69, 78, 83–6, 88, 97–8, 101–2,
  112, 120

Jacob 78, 97, 101
Jebusites 101
Jeroboam II 124
Jesse 3
Jesus 3, 124 n.16
Joab 120 n.10
Job 58–60, 118
Joseph 119
Judah 78, 101, 119

---

* The indices catalogue scriptural texts and scriptural characters outside of, rather than within, the book of Jonah.

136   *Scriptural Characters Index*

Kadmonites 101
Kenites 101
Kenizzites 101

land, the 19, 20, 22–3, 28, 39, 44, 68–9,
    72, 83, 84, 87, 91, 95–7, 98, 99,
      101–3, 107, 119, 120, 122, 125
Leviathan 59–62
Levite(s) 78, 112

Mahlon 98
Malik 125 n.17
Micah 35 n.1, 101–2
Moab(ite) 88, 98, 102, 119
Mohammed 67, 105 n.4
Moses 27, 46, 77, 83–6, 89

Naboth 40
Nahum 8, 35, 78, 124
Naomi 98, 99, 102, 119
Nephilim 82
Noah 46, 63, 83, 84, 112

Orpah 99

Palestine 69, 81
Perizzites 101
Pharaohs 88 n.4
Philistines 49 n.6
poor, the 10, 45
Priest 73

Rachel 102
Rahab 40, 98 n.9
redeemer, the 98 n.9,
    119
Rephaim 101
robbers 73
Ruth 2, 98–9, 102, 119

Samaritan, the 73
Samuel 84, 86, 89
Sarah 98
  Sarai 98–9, 101, 102,
    120 n.9
Saul 83–4, 86, 89, 114, 120
serpent, the 61 n.5, 62,
    94, 106
Shechem 71
Sodom and Gomorrah 78
Solomon 37, 39, 117

Tamar 119
Tanin 61 n.5, 62
tree of life 5, 106
Tselem 57 n.3

Uriah 120 n.10
Ur of Chaldea 98

wicked, the 94, 95

Yūnus 67

SCRIPTURAL REFERENCE INDEX

Genesis
1	81
1.1	56
1.1-2	31
1.2	57
1.9-10	31, 34, 57
1.11	57, 58
1.12	57
1.13	57
1.24	57
1.24-25	56, 58
1.25	57
1.26	57, 58
1.27-28	46
1.28-28	57 n.3
1.29-30	36
2–3	25, 38, 81
2.4b-7	58
2.4b–3.24	106
2.7	20
3.1	62
3.5b	62
3.6	34
3.14a	62
3.17b–18	39
4.3	39
4.3-4	58 n.4
4.17	78
6–7	37
6–9	82
6.1-5	82
6.5-8	62
6.5b-6	82
6.6-7	46
6.11-16	46
6.17	46
7	46
7.2	63
7.12	37
8	46
8.20	63
8.21b	82, 83

9.1-17	46
9.9	83
9.9-17	83
9.11	83
9.16	83
11.1-9	78
11.30	98
12	39
12.5	98
13.2	64
13.7	64
15	98
15.18-21	101
16	98
16.13	47
17.14	49 n.6
19	37
19.1-11	119
19.30-38	102
21.1-8	98
22	38
34.2	71
34.23	64
35.19	102
36.3	64
37.12-28	11 n.8
38.12-19	119
41.7	94
41.46-49	119
42	119

Exodus
2.23-4	97
3.2-3	77
4.1-17	89
4.10-17	83
7.12	94
12	37
8.17-18	64
15.12	94
19.18	77
22.18	63

32	39, 83, 84, 86, 87
32.4b	83
32.9-13	46
32.10	84
32.11-14	84
32.14	46

Leviticus
11.39	63
18.23	63
18.25	95
18.28	95
20.15-16	63
20.22	95

Numbers
14.33-34	37
16.30	94
22–24	88, 106
22.28	106

Deuteronomy
8.2 38	

Joshua
2	40, 88, 98 n.9
6	37
10.12-15	37

Judges
14.3	49 n.6
19.16-21	119

Ruth
1.1	98
1.6-7	99
1.8	99
1.9-10	99
1.11-13	99
3.13	119
4	119

Scriptural Reference Index

4.1-6	119	40.15-18	60	*Ezekiel*	
4.6	119	40.15-24	58, 59	4	89
		40.19	59, 62	27.12	21
1 Samuel		40.19b	60	27.25	117
7.7-9	89	40.19-22	60		
15.11	83, 89	40.23	60	*Micah*	
17.16	37	40.24	60	5.1	101
26.5	114	40.25-32	59		
28.15-19	89	40.26	60	*Nahum*	
31.1-7	89	40.31	59	3.5b	78
		40.32	59		
2 Samuel		41	59	*Matthew*	
1.1-10	89	41.2	59	12.40	124 n.16
5.4	37			26.39	119
11–12	39	*Psalms*			
11.4	71	21.9	94	*Luke*	
11.14-15	120 n.10	23	46	10.25-37	73
		26.2	38	10.36	73
1 Kings		35	46	10.37	73
5	117	48.7	117		
10.22	21	69.15	94	*John*	
11.1-13	39	72.10	21	15.5	3
11.42	37	74.12-17	60		
18.41-46	37	74.14	59, 60,	*Qur'an*	
21	40		62	1.1	71, 80
		104.26	59	4.163	105 n.4
2 Kings		139	46	6.86	105 n.4
14.23-29	124			10.98	67, 89
14.25	20	*Ecclesiastes*		37.139	121
		10.12	94	37.139-140	116
Job				37.139-142	104
2.10	118	*Isaiah*		37.140	105 n.6
3–31	59	2.16	117	37.140-141	93
3.8	59	11.1	3	37.142-144	92
8.18	94	21.1	59	37.143	70
10.8	94	27.1	59, 61, 62	37.145	103
20.15	95	60.9	118	37.145-146	68
32–37	59			37.147	67, 89
38	59	*Jeremiah*		37.147-148	66, 73
40	61 n.5	10.9	21		
40.1-5	59				

www.ingramcontent.com/pod-product-compliance
Ingram Content Group UK Ltd.
Pitfield, Milton Keynes, MK11 3LW, UK
UKHW021541050225
4464UKWH00031B/503